The Touring Vegan

By Jon Siren

"This book is a window into the rarely exposed world of a touring vegan drummer that is and was in a bunch of great bands. Amazing stories, awesome reflections, and fantastic tips on super healthy veganism from a dude that walks the walk."

-Vegan Black Metal Chef

Preface

When I first started writing this book I simply wanted to present the challenges I faced when traveling as a vegan musician. My goal was to share my pitfalls and the solutions I came up with while traveling in this alternative lifestyle. I never intended to spend so much time focusing on why I decided to embark on a vegan path or the arguments favoring this lifestyle.

In the recent years, there has been a social shift towards veganism in the advent of popular documentaries on Netflix such as "What The Health," "Forks Over Knives" and "Cowspiracy." Restaurants, supermarkets, clothing stores and various institutions have recognized this shift and have been slowly accommodating the demands of their cruelty-free consumers. This is a monumental victory for myself and other vegans out there who were fighting an uphill battle on a daily basis because of our decision to break from the status quo. It has caused a surge of support groups online who share their own unique stories of how they maintain this lifestyle in a world that isn't set-up to accommodate this way of living.

Being vegan wasn't nearly as easy when I started back in Columbus, Ohio in the mid-90's. This book is about my journey of discovering this lifestyle and my struggles maintaining it over the years, with a heavy focus on how I do this when preparing for a tour and embarking on a tour.

With the internet and websites like YouTube, the philosophies and scientific studies favoring this lifestyle are a lot easier to access. Doctors, philosophers and everyday people can share their stories, provide information and interact instantly. I'm still blown away by the ease of gathering information in the 21st century. One would have to go to a library or find a health food store where they can get a pamphlet or one or two books on the subject. Becoming vegan is easier than ever and I hope that this book inspires a few people and also helps fellow touring musicians who want to maintain this lifestyle while on the road.

This book is for entertainment only. I am not a medical professional and one should always consult a medical professional before changing their diet.

Chapter 1
My Beginning

Growing up in Columbus, Ohio in the 1980's, I had what seemed to be the typical American diet. For breakfast, I enjoyed Count Chocula cereal with chocolate milk, and Hi-C Ecto Cooler. Ecto Cooler was a neon green colored drink with artificial orange flavoring and 100% of my daily supply of vitamin-C added. My mom always stressed the importance of having Vitamin C to help make sure that I wouldn't get sick. For lunch, it would be whatever the school cafeteria offered, which probably hasn't changed much and in some places. It may have gotten worse with fast food companies setting up shop at schools. Lunch was usually something like spaghetti with meat sauce, a salad bar with anemic iceberg lettuce, pale carrot shreds and a flavorless tomato wedge. The dressing choices were of the standard variety: French, Italian, 1000 Island or Ranch. That didn't matter. Most of us didn't eat salad anyway. We would then have some sort of pre-packaged snack cake for desert. We all had our choice of whole milk, skim milk or artificial orange drink. Skim milk was the rage back then, so most of us with parents who were trying to set us on the proper path encouraged us to drink the skim milk. I never really snacked much as a child while at school. It wasn't until we were older and my diet changed that our school introduced vending machines with candy bars, chips, and sodas. After school, I would usually eat a meal that my mom would prepare. My favorite, (and a classic at our house,) was frozen fish sticks, frozen fries, and frozen corn. All were warmed up in either the microwave or toaster oven, and I would drink more milk for my mealtime beverage. Milk seemed like the healthiest food on the planet because there were constantly commercials on TV and our parents would stress the importance of the calcium in milk for making our bones strong. After dinner, I might snack on something. We kept a lot of cookies, chips and sodas around for us to feast on while my brother, sister, and I did our homework.

Reflecting back on what we ate, I cringe a bit because it goes against everything I would learn later on in regards to health and ethics. I don't blame my family or my school because this was very normal for a lot of families that I grew up around. Most people's idea of healthy eating was simply obeying the 4 food groups, and one could easily do so having canned vegetables, potato chips, lunch-meat slices, ice cream, and bottled fruit juices. Quality of those foods wasn't stressed as much, at least not in my world. The concept of eating whole food and less processed food wasn't widely understood then. There were probably only a few children that I grew up around that had home cooked meals without tons of added fat or sodium, made with whole foods. We'll get more into health and food philosophy later.

I ate like this day in and day out for a while. As a young boy, I noticed I would have sinus congestion often. I was always tired and sick. I didn't really make any sort of association between what I ate and how I felt. When I was a teenager, my parents started having problems and my dad moved out. The changes at home led to me taking care of myself more. This unfortunate event forced me to learn how to start preparing my own meals because my mother had to start going to school again and began working. I remember my mom showing me how to make stir-fried chicken with vegetables from a frozen box and I usually ate that or those frozen fish sticks when I came home from school. I did have a bit of excitement building up in me during these difficult times when preparing my own meals. I'm not sure if it was my independence or if it was an excitement that I got because I was creating something and was fascinated by the art of cooking. Either way, it was the silver lining during this time and sparked a bit of culinary interest.

I'll rewind a bit in life back to when I was around six or seven years old. Around this time, I wanted a pet so badly. I really wanted a dog but I think that was probably too much work for my parents, so the family opted for guinea pigs instead. I loved my guinea pigs. I named mine "Teddy" and my sister had one named "Cher." The guinea pigs were the first vegetarians I had ever met as well as being my first pets. I'd feed them a diet of cabbage, carrots, and those alfalfa pellets that pet rodents and rats eat. I would always bring them out of the cage to sit with me, as I'd watch MTV. That's right; I was watching MTV around six years old. I remember a babysitter always watching it as well as an older friend from the neighborhood. I was so enthralled by the images and the sound - I was hooked! So instead of watching Sesame Street and cartoons as a child, I preferred MTV. My guinea pigs would sit on the couch with me. Sometimes they weren't the most graceful animals and would simply fall off the side and then start squealing loudly in what seemed like a lot of pain. It upset me so much to see these fragile creatures feel pain that I did whatever I could to protect them from it. After they'd fall off the couch a couple of times, I was sure to plant my body on the edge, so that they couldn't fall anymore. Guinea pigs generally don't live too long, but ours did. I think they were six or seven years old when they finally passed and I was absolutely devastated. It was a while before I had more animals in my life. From this a seed was planted and began to slowly grow.

One thing that I loved doing as a child was to go fishing. This started with my Uncle Jim out off the coast of New Jersey at a young age, also around six or seven. My dad would take me fishing as well, back in Ohio in some of the creeks and rivers nearby. I begged him to do so after these trips with my uncle. I loved spending this time bonding with them and it was always fun catching the fish. We mostly just let them go because a lot of what we caught was too small to eat. However, there was one time that I caught a pretty large flounder when fishing with my uncle. He decided to keep it along with a couple of others he caught. When we got back to his place with the fish, he told me we had to clean them first before we had them for dinner. I was very apprehensive about this. At the time, I didn't see what we were doing as anything bad up until that point. Uncle Jim took the first fish and cut its head off right out of the water bucket we had it in. The blood and the flapping around of the fish were horrifying to me as the fish was dying. He then proceeded to scale and filet the fish. I was in tears when he handed me the knife to do the same with the fish that I had caught. I couldn't do it. I ran inside to where my aunt was starting to prepare the rest of the meal and stayed with her. This was the end of my fishing journey.

As my childhood progressed, I had a number of occurrences that caused conflicted feelings when it came to eating meat. At the same time, I never knew a vegetarian or heard much about vegetarianism. I can recall always feeling bad anytime I saw or heard an animal in pain and it always made me uncomfortable when I'd see a human disciplining an animal physically in public places. I think the worst examples of animal abuse that I witnessed as a child was when I made the mistake of renting the movie "Faces of Death." "Faces of Death" is a series of movies that some movie rental places carried in the horror section. It contained raw footage of people and animals dying, usually in brutal ways. There were many suicides and car accidents on film as well. In addition to that, there were plenty of animal experimentations, slaughterhouse scenes of cows, chickens, and pigs getting beaten to death, (especially when the bolt guns that they used failed to work,) and clubbing of baby seals for their hides. It is absolutely terrifying stuff to watch as an adult, let alone as a child, and it certainly had a lasting effect on me. I knew at an early age that I wanted to protect animals that were easily dominated by humans, but I hadn't known or thought of my own eating habits until that last time I went fishing with my uncle. I don't think any of our parents knew what this movie was, so I don't think many of them thought of how disturbing the content was. It was lined up next to Clive Barker and Wes Craven films on the shelves in video stores. The mainstream chains would never carry these films. Today, you can probably access even more disturbing footage than this, and everyday sites such as YouTube have footage of slaughterhouses and fur farms. Maybe this animal torture imagery has caused a larger awareness of what we consume regularly. I know the whole world isn't ready for veganism but I do see a lot more "faux fur and leather" out there and less of the real stuff because most sensible people out there think owning a fur coat is just barbaric and unnecessary. Meat, on the other hand, is something that people on a large scale aren't ready to give up. However, I feel that most people I come across would like to see the farm animals treated better, and are usually appalled when viewing slaughterhouse footage or when they see chickens crammed into cages covered in their own filth. It bothers us to see this sort of thing, even those who haven't made any decision to change.

I was quite religious growing up. I was raised Catholic by my mother and I went to church every Sunday. I admit that it helped shape my moral code to some degree even though I have moved from my former faith. Certain concepts stuck with me and so did some of my interpretations of what was being taught. I remember the Ten Commandments well and "Thou Shall Not Kill" started to really resonate strongly with me, as did the golden rule of "Do unto others as you would have them do unto you." Something wasn't feeling right with the way I was living, and I hadn't quite figured out why or what it was, but slowly I was moving towards a lifestyle change. More key events began happening in my life that helped this transformation move along quicker.

My childhood, like most childhoods, was a very confusing time. I really struggled with finding my path in life and listened to a lot of music to escape the horrible feelings I had within me. I lacked self-confidence. I went from being a child who excelled in sports to someone who couldn't compete on the same level as my peers who were developing faster. I think being a late bloomer had some negative effects on me at the time, and I started moving away from being a swimmer and springboard diver. I was also having constant friction with my sister and parents. The animosity within our house really wore me out and made me want to distance myself as much as I could in all ways.

I was about 16 years old when my father committed suicide. That may have been the single most difficult part of my life and with it came a radical change within me. Coupled with that, within about a two year time period surrounding that event, I'd lost both grandparents on my mom's side, my uncle and my sister. My sister died in a car accident shortly after my dad's death and all of this death really shook things up. I needed a change.

I wanted more than anything to be seen and to be heard. I think that is why I eventually chose the path of being a musician. Music was the only thing that made sense to me during my turbulent youth. I was air guitaring in front of the mirror as Guns N' Roses videos played on MTV. I thought that if these crazy looking outcasts with awesome songs could rise above the masses and be accepted in the world than maybe there is some sort of hope for me to do the same.

I didn't dive in "head first" though. I was never a great musician and I bounced around between instruments before finding my love of the drums. I didn't have the ability to focus on practicing. I just wanted the results without putting in the time, and I can't say I was gifted with talent either. I think maybe I was too devastated by my home life to really have a focused plan in life or to spend time honing my craft on an instrument. I also hated piano growing up. In an attempt for me to be a well-rounded child, my mom forced me to take piano lessons each week. I never practiced and my first impression of learning an instrument wasn't any fun for me. I wouldn't practice and as a result, I would get an earful from both my mother and the piano teacher each week because I wasn't progressing. When I finally got to play an instrument that made sense to me like "the guitar" I did the same thing though. I hated the lessons. I wasn't interested in the type of music that was being taught to me and so I failed at it.

I'm surprised that I convinced them to buy me a bass guitar after these failed attempts at music lessons. For some reason bass seemed so cool. Watching White Lion videos made me so excited by the bass guitar. I remember the bassist having this awesome red bass in the "Tell Me" video and he was running all around, looking badass. I also heard that it was easier than guitar and my thoughts at the time were, "ok, so if I play the bass, it is something that is needed in a band and its easier than guitar, so I'll definitely get to be in a band some day because most kids I know want to be a singer or a guitarist." Nobody around me liked the bass, but we all knew it was necessary. To take things a step further, I did want to play drums all along but that took years of convincing my parents to allow this to happen. They knew that drums were super loud and that with a guitar or bass you could just turn the amplifier down and everyone would be happy. I did eventually get to play the drums, but at the time, I excelled a bit more on the bass because of the experience I had up to that point. Also, some of the older kids in school would have these jam sessions and nobody played bass, so I was always invited to jam with the kids that were a bit more experienced and that helped me to learn as a result.

I spent the next few middle school years dabbling with bass and drums but mostly I would just listen to music on MTV and hang out in a nearby record store that specialized in underground music like death metal, punk and industrial. Most of my practice came from listening to bands as opposed to playing scales on my bass or paradiddles "a standard rudiment" on my drums.

During this time in high school, I remember having my first vegetarian meal. I was at my friend Amy's house along with a couple of other friends from school. She cooked us all a vegetarian meal, which was so difficult to wrap my head around. There wasn't any meat! I thought I was going to starve when we sat down. I remember it well. She made some sort of pasta with a cream sauce and we had some assorted cooked vegetables and a salad. I felt like I needed two helpings to get full. I'm not sure if it was a good or bad experience. It certainly challenged my idea of what a meal should be. I thought I would need to get Taco Bell on the way home in order to satisfy my need for meat. Meat was always considered the centerpiece to every meal. I had never come across anyone who challenged this and was surprised at the experience that I had. I always remembered that meal though. Amy and another friend Laura were both vegetarians and I found that to be fascinating. I may have made fun of them about it, as teenagers would, but I also found it kind of cool in some way. I just couldn't wrap my head around it all yet.

During my quest for truth and answers in life, I listened to a lot of music. Music was my life. It still is today! It was my answer to anything and it was fitting for any situation but mostly for my dark moments. It is something that I want to either listen to or perform at any hour of the day. There is always a song that fits the moment with me. I think because of my turbulent upbringing and unstable home life, my musical tastes were always dark or heavy or both. My musical pallet reflected my feelings of sadness, anger, and a desire for some sort of justice in life. I wanted to rise above my situation and feel a sense of freedom that I would get from playing music as my livelihood. I was very much against all forms of oppression, be it to a human or an animal, and I needed to hear music that was aggressive and immediate with its delivery. A band didn't need to be outright political to muster up the feelings that I'd identify with. I didn't even necessarily have to always understand the lyrics. My favorite genre in my early teens was death metal, which usually didn't have any sort of political agenda. If anything it had nihilistic lyrics that you couldn't understand, but I identified with the intensity of the delivery.

I had my favorite bands for every feeling that I was going through, but one band in particular stood out and really helped me to change my path in life. That band was Earth Crisis. Earth Crisis was the first vegan, straight edge, hardcore band that I had ever heard. They had a powerful message with music that was as heavy as Slayer's to back it up. Here were these guys from Syracuse, NY touring around the Midwest with pamphlets from PETA (People for the Ethical Treatment of Animals) and other animal rights groups, playing music that got their audiences going berserk in the pit. I was sold. I think they were just the kind of push that I needed to start feeling better and head down a path that made sense to me and not the direction that I may have been heading. Through Earth Crisis, I discovered other bands with a similar message and approach. I quickly became part of the whole hardcore movement of the early 90's. I started to feel like I had a purpose and was helping to make the world a better place. I was part of a movement that had a positive agenda, executed in a way that spoke to me as well as thousands of other disenfranchised teens.

Declaring myself to be a vegan in Columbus, Ohio around 1994 was not the easiest thing to do. I had just a handful of pamphlets from PETA and I came across the only book in the bookstore on the subject called "Simply Vegan." The book centered a lot of its meals around soy products, which was this mysterious thing to me, and something that I couldn't easily access back then. I didn't know what TVP (Textured Vegetable Protein) was or seitan (wheat meat) or even what tofu was. I had a bad idea of tofu because that was what hippies ate who were getting ready for a Grateful Dead show. I was an angry metalhead and Grateful Dead fans from my high school made fun of me a lot and so I cringed at the idea of tofu. I thought that was a hippy Grateful Dead sort of thing. Ahh, youth. I can't ignore that this was my thought process though. I struggled hard. I can remember some of my first meals being cans of vegetarian baked-beans with corn tortilla chips. I just had no clue on how to do this at all in a healthy way. I tried to find some of these "mock meats" that I heard about but a lot of them in the grocery store near me still contained dairy or egg products. They were vegetarian but not hard-core vegan which was what I was striving for. It was tough doing this with limited culinary knowledge and a lot of preconceived ideas of what healthy cuisine meant. I didn't care though, I finally felt that I was living life the way I should by obeying that golden rule and following the Ten Commandments, but including animals as well with the "Thou shall not kill" concept. It just felt right on a moral level to rid myself of consuming animal products.

Shortly into my newly found vegan lifestyle, I had a falling out with the church. As much as I agreed with some of the basic principles of how to treat others, I had issues with the church's reluctance on providing my dad with a burial service because of the suicide. I started to see some of the hypocritical ways that people within the church behaved. I thought that they weren't really living by the golden rule that they pushed for so many years in Sunday school and in sermons. This only brought about more feelings of wanting to find justice and truth in life, a quest that continues on today. I remember some of my Sunday school class discussions, I'd bring up veganism and I was told by many of the teachers that animals were there for us to eat and that "Thou Shall Not Kill" only applies to humans. This didn't resonate well with me. I further distanced myself from religious institutions, until I eventually stopped attending and opted for science to explain the mysteries of life.

I think the hardcore scene that I immersed myself in acted in a similar way the church once did for me. It was a combination of music, camaraderie, and politics "dealing with animal rights and social justice." We had several "hardcore houses" that would host bands, vegan potlucks and other events such as "Food Not Bombs" which gathered on Sundays to cook vegan food that was donated by co-ops for the homeless.

I think this really helped me feel like I had a place in life and a purpose because I didn't identify with most of the people I went to school with or my family. It helped inspire some of my first bands "Medium" and "Inept," both putting out albums that were heavy with a vegan and socially conscious message. It was with these bands that I first got my taste of touring.

Being vegan in the hardcore scene was common, so when we'd play shows with other bands, getting fed vegan food was something that would often happen. Money was tight, so vegan or not, options were limited. If an out of town band was playing, we might make the group spaghetti with tomato sauce, which would cost under $5 to feed 4 or 5 people. That was a normal meal for a touring band. We all had to fend for ourselves throughout the day though. Nobody I knew approached things in a health conscious manner back then. We were more concerned with the cost and whether or not the meal could fill us up. Bread and peanut butter were common food rations while on tour as well. Both items were cheap, vegan and filling. We also ate a lot of "soda crackers" with our peanut butter because we knew those were vegan and the ingredient list wasn't a mile long with additives potentially derived from animal products.

Occasionally, we'd eat an apple or some fruit if we could. Vegans back then in the hardcore scene seemed sickly to outsiders (and I even thought so, too) because we didn't approach things with health as a priority. There was more literature out there bashing this lifestyle than promoting it, so we all felt the uphill battle. There simply wasn't enough research or resources to help people that desired to approach food differently.

I do recall a vegan straightedge group called "Hardline" who put out 'zines promoting radical veganism. This group of vegans were all for direct action of destroying fur farms and factory farms and they seemed to have a manifesto of building vegan soldiers. Their literature would often include ways to be really healthy being vegan with instructions on how to lift weights so that one could be a strong representation of the group. There were also a lot of nutrition articles to help keep the vegans on the path they were on, to help defy the stereotypes that vegans were these anemic weaklings. My friends and other kids in this scene frowned upon this radical group of vegans, probably because we were as isolated as we were when we'd be around our schoolmates and regular everyday people. The Hardline kids were even more extreme and were often isolated as well, even among vegans within the scene. If I think about their 'zines and ideas now, they don't seem as radical. So many vegan people approach the lifestyle in a holistic way and the only thing that may seem radical to some is the direct action that the Hardline kids encouraged. Many vegans today focus on health a lot more because a picture is worth a thousand words. Therefore, most vegans that I know are concerned with how they look physically because they know this is the best way they can promote this lifestyle.

As my journey evolved, I began to learn how to feed myself a little better. I learned how to really cook around the time I was 17 years old from doing these "Food Not Bombs" events and from my high school girlfriend, Ada, and her mom. Before that, I was merely preparing 2-step dishes such as veggie burgers on bread with potato chips or spaghetti with marinara sauce. Ada and her family were from Poland and they were staying in the US for a couple of years because of her father's job. She didn't grow up with the same sort of diets we had in the US at that time. In fact, because of the political climate of the 80's in Poland, they had to deal with food shortages all of the time. Much of what they ate was a few root vegetables made into soups such as borscht, buckwheat groats, potatoes, (usually in the form of pierogies,) and dark, dense bread with a few condiments such as sour cream. Processed food and a variety of ingredients were not common among working class families and the poor. Most people ate a very simple, whole foods diet. I was lucky that Ada just happened to be a vegetarian, so she taught me the basics of cooking. I learned how to make borscht (beet soup), buckwheat kasha and potato pancakes from her. We also ate a ton of fake meat. Fake meat seems to be big with people transitioning over to veganism from a meat-centered diet and I wasn't any different. Also, as the economy got better in Poland, adding sausage to meals was very common. Instead of eating sausage, I'd eat soy or wheat-based sausage. I felt that I needed that dense calorie concoction derived from wheat and soy at most of my meals as I started to prepare more evolved dishes for myself.

During the early 90's in Columbus, we didn't have the vast array of plant-based meats and cheeses that one can find in most grocery stores today. At the time, there was only one frozen vegan burger that I could find nearby my place and I would buy most of the inventory anytime I went to the grocery store. A couple of natural food co-ops began to pop up in the late 90's and my options for processed and prepackaged vegan foods began to expand. There were now plenty of frozen veggie burgers, hot dogs, vegan Indian and Thai frozen meals, vegan soups, and even vegan desserts such as cookies and soy ice cream. We were getting to an age where one could find just about any animal-based packaged food in a vegan form.

Time moved forward and I became more and more comfortable with my transition now that I had a few meal concepts under my belt and a good support system of people who also felt a similar way. A lot of these hardcore kids worked at the one vegetarian restaurant in town too, and I felt so happy the day that I got a job washing dishes there. I figured I'd at least be in the kitchen and I could taste and see all of the amazing dishes they came up with, thus broadening my horizons as far as eating goes. The food was revolutionary to me. I often thought to myself, if I could eat like this every day, I'd exude health and vitality and I could show others how easy it is to be vegan. I remember the seitan (wheat meat) gyro with tomato basil couscous being the best thing on the planet! They also had a watercress sandwich with vegan cream cheese, chipotle chili, and a few other amazing dishes that were made fresh daily. I was such an enthusiastic employee there that my boss moved me up the ladder in the kitchen quickly. At one point I became his assistant chef.

A lot was happening by the time I was eighteen years old and figuring out what to do about college and my future. I didn't think too much about where I'd go when considering options. There had been other unfortunate events in my life like my sister dying in a car crash shortly after my father's death. I didn't really want to leave town and not be around my mother who was also going through a rough time. I ended up at Ohio State University and switched my major about three or four times within a year because I couldn't figure out what I was going to do. My mom always stressed that I need a career that would pay for what I need in life. Music should be played on weekends and be a secondary focus unless I was wanting to teach in the school system and make a steady career with music. On some level, I agreed and I didn't fight it because it seemed like sound advice. I never really learned how to play my instruments well anyway, so majoring in music wasn't going to happen.

The major that I stuck with the longest was "Social Work." I figured that I'd try to help people in life who needed it as my career. With my growing knowledge working at the local vegetarian restaurant, I had to do some volunteer work for my social work major at a runaway shelter in Columbus. I helped teenagers, mostly only a year younger than me, learn how to cook their own meals. My diet at the time was controversial when brought up amongst the vast population and I thought there was no way they'd want me teaching kids about veganism. To my surprise, they were totally cool with me showing them how to make a few simple meals that I knew how to make without using meat. I even came across a few teens that were vegetarian or vegan themselves which made my work easier. As much as I enjoyed helping out and following the "social work" path, it wasn't exactly my calling. At least it wasn't the route I wanted to take to get from A to B even though it had given me some of the fulfillment I was maybe looking for by helping others. I wanted to make a difference in people's lives but in a different way.

While in college, I joined the "University Band for Non-Music Majors." Maybe this was a bit of wishful thinking or foreshadowing, but I thought that if I showed any skill here, it would be something I could pursue professionally as either a music teacher or a performer. I had a pretty good time in the percussion section but compared to the other players out there, I struggled to pull my own weight. I was usually put on bass drum or auxiliary percussion (cymbals, triangle, shakers). These types of positions were usually for the weaker players and involved a tremendous amount of counting rests instead of actually playing. Then, I'd have that one key moment, one hundred bars in, where I'd hit the triangle once! Hey, somebody has got to do it. One time, I must have dozed off and I came in at the wrong time and managed to train wreck the band because I threw the conductor off. He sat down with me later and asked what I wanted to major in. When I told him I was thinking about music, he gave me a confused look that I'll never forget. He was a good guy and meant well, but he had that look that read something like "you really missed the boat on that, good luck." I remember feeling a little heartbroken from that moment, but I felt determined to prove him wrong. I had no idea if I'd graduate with a degree in music or not, but I wasn't about to be a quitter.

Maybe it was a lasting impression that my father left on me before he took his life, that I was so determined to follow my passion at all costs. I think he lived with a lot of regret. I think he really wanted to follow his passion of photography but entered a more stable career path as a radiologist. My impression was that he felt stuck with his life and wished that maybe he took a chance at something more artistic. I felt more of a drive now to not repeat his same mistakes. I had to start heading in a direction that made sense to me even if the odds were stacked against me.

Life was getting stagnant for me in Columbus, Ohio. When reading through a Vegetarian Times magazine about a five month chef's training program in New York City that focused on vegan cooking, I made the decision to head there to pursue a career in cooking. I wanted to make my mother happy. With a culinary background, my chances of finding steady work to support my needs would be greater than life as a touring musician in hardcore bands, something I was recently experiencing on a small scale.

During my last year of high school and my first year of college, my bands managed to do a lot of one to two week tours during holiday breaks and summers. We'd play house parties in other cities and swap gigs with different bands by providing each other with places to play in each other's hometowns. We had an awesome time doing it, but we didn't have much success finding large audiences or making much money. It was truly a labor of love. We often had to dip into our own pockets in order to support our love for traveling and performing. This all factored in with my decision to move out of Columbus and pursue a more stable path. My first dose of the music business was a harsh lesson that I looked at more as an expensive hobby. I figured since I really enjoyed cooking professionally, maybe by going to school I could make more of a career out of it, even though music was still my number one love. I let fear guide me on this move but I don't necessarily regret it. I have learned a lot of valuable skills that I still employ daily. I can always prepare healthy meals for myself and I don't have to resort to spending extra money at the grocery store buying expensive, less healthy, prepackaged meals. This skill is worth its weight in gold to me.

While in New York, I took up a couple of jobs. One was at a vegan bakery and the other was at a raw vegan restaurant. I felt the need to broaden my horizons in the vegan culinary world. It was so crazy to be in a city where there were such niche vegan restaurants and a number of them to boot. There were vegan Ethiopian, Korean, Thai and Indian places as well as vegan café's, fine dining and greasy spoons. NYC was most definitely at the forefront of vegan culture in the 90's.

At school, I didn't feel like I was learning much because I had been reading a lot on my own and my head chef back in Columbus was such a skilled cook. He really set me up with the fundamentals necessary to work professionally. I had been trained on the job how to use knives properly, how to prepare staple dishes and he helped me to develop my food pallet as well. I felt that I was starting from the ground up while I was there instead of mastering my craft and exploring deeper into the culinary world.

My interests seemed to head back to music while in this culinary program and maybe one of the reasons had to do with the ease of the classes that I was involved in. While there, I was starting to feel that maybe cooking wasn't really what I wanted in life. It was a bit of a dilemma because I'd spent a good amount of money getting out to NYC and paying for school, but I didn't feel like I was getting a whole lot out of it. I was having regrets and doubts about my decision. I was also greatly influenced by a book that I picked up called "The Sunfood

Diet Success System" by David Wolfe. This was a food philosophy book that encouraged a raw vegan diet. In other words, it encouraged a diet based on uncooked plant food for ethical reasons and for the belief that raw, unprocessed food is what humans are designed to eat exclusively.

I was so unfocused in my early 20's and teens that I was in this vegan culinary program, yet I was moving into an even more niche group of veganism that only consumed raw foods. What would I possibly learn from school if I were having this radical change in belief systems? Raw foods was something that was touched on in the program as sort of a temporarily healing diet but surely wasn't a focus. They were training us to be professional chefs in vegan restaurants or the private chef world. I was learning how to cook but wanting to just eat food in its raw, natural state after being sucked into the philosophy of Wolfe's book. I could see that my options of work following this niche lifestyle would be extremely limited upon graduating the program if I continued down this path. I became even more isolated because of my evolving food philosophy. The idea behind a raw vegan is that humans are the only animals that cook their own food and, for optimal health, we should be eating the way we did before discovering fire. I still think there is a lot of merit behind the food philosophy of the raw vegan and I believe that one can maintain excellent health if done in the right way. I don't think I was doing this in the optimal way because I focused on eating a ton of nuts for my calories and to feel satiated, something that will probably make anyone fail on this lifestyle because of the amount of fat that is in a serving of nuts. When one eats mostly nuts as the centerpiece of their diet, it tends to lead to feeling lethargic and bloated. I continued with this philosophy while in NYC but later on in life, I moved more towards a whole foods vegan lifestyle that incorporates both raw and cooked foods.

In the meantime, I was again putting my life's path in question. Did I want to cook food professionally for people when my philosophy behind food was changing or did I want to follow another path? It was back to the drawing board for me. I couldn't see myself going back to Ohio and trying to re-enroll in a more traditional major. It simply wasn't me and I knew that it would lead to unhappiness in life. I think my father's regret of not pursuing photography resonated within me and so I made the decision that I was going to try to enroll in music school.

The most fun I ever had in life was going to shows, watching MTV and performing in these hardcore bands. I felt that if I was doing something on that level, but made enough to put food on the table and a roof over my head, then everything would be perfect. I was regretting not paying attention or being as focused during music lessons as a young boy and wondered if it was too late to really push for a career in music which was still something that I felt my mother wouldn't really approve of.

Through a buddy of mine back in Columbus who was a great jazz musician, I asked if he knew any teachers in NYC that could help me out. Luckily, he did. While balancing two jobs and school, I started taking drum lessons. This time, I really focused and I told the teacher that I wanted to try to get into music school. He had been through school himself and started showing me how to read music charts, how to sight read, how to play the basics when it comes to jazz, Afro-Cuban, funk and other modern styles that music schools focus on. I learned a lot in a short amount of time with him, I had a used electronic drum kit in my tiny Brooklyn apartment where I started practicing for hours as soon as I got home from either work or school. I lived right over a subway entrance, so with all of the noise in the area, my racket didn't seem to bother my neighbors. I may have secretly annoyed my roommate, but fortunately, he didn't say anything to me or object to my practicing.

I didn't get out much during my time in NYC but I did happen to check out this industrial metal band that I had seen in Columbus about a year earlier called "Kevorkian Death Cycle." They were awesome! I had never seen a band combine electronic synthesizer sounds with guitars and heavy drums. I went down to CBGB's "RIP" and attended their show. When they hit the stage, I noticed quickly that there was no drummer this time! I was shocked! I wanted to stop the show, grab my kit and offer to join right then and there. I had been practicing to their albums for fun already, so I was very familiar with the beats. As soon as their show ended, I boldly went up to the keyboardist, Roger, and asked him what happened to their drummer. He gave me a story as to why he had to leave the tour and they said that they were able to finish the tour without him using the electronic drum samples from the albums as a backing track. I saw an opportunity and I told him that I'm a drummer and we hit it off right there. He offered me to try out for the band back in Redlands, California (a suburb far from the Los Angeles area) once they returned home from tour.

There was a fire brewing inside me. The thought of being a touring drummer of a band that I idolized really got me to practice rigorously every day. I know it is tough to do it all but I was having a great time cooking at these vegan establishments and developing my skills on the drums. I was closer to my goal in life, which was to find a path that made sense to me doing what I love without any compromise - or with as little as possible. I also wanted to make enough money doing it so that I'd get my mom's approval, and so that my passion could be my livelihood. I say "livelihood" because it sounds better than "job." A job sounds negative, like something we have to do whereas "livelihood" encompasses the idea of "job" but in such a way that sounds positive and exciting. Getting to drum for a living doesn't sound like a job but a livelihood. I think it is important that we all find something in life that we love so much, where we can earn some money to live on as well, and make it our focus to achieve this. I'm excited everyday to practice or play a show. I may worry about money because the music industry has been very unstable for me, but how lucky am I now to be able to do what I love? Ok, time to get back on track.

I stayed in touch with Roger and scheduled a time to fly out to the Los Angeles area to meet up with him and try out. When I showed up and met with the band, I was nervous but managed to play the parts and they appeared to like what I was doing. They didn't tell me if I got the gig or not though. I stayed in touch with Roger and he seemed like he was trying to figure out how I could make the move out there and work while playing with the band. I don't think there was a lot of money in touring with an industrial metal band unless you were Rammstein, so one would need to supplement one's income somehow. So much thought was racing through my head at the time. I hadn't quite settled into NYC and I was only scheduled to be there the five months and then, we'd see what chapter opens next. I decided that I'd try to get into a music school and finish my degree while possibly drumming for Kevorkian Death Cycle.

My drum teacher prepared me for the audition at Musicians Institute in Los Angeles and I managed to get into their newly formed degree program. MI was considered a vocational school up until that point but they partnered up with Los Angeles City College to create a bachelors in music program into which I had proudly been accepted. Also, I wouldn't have to take any general education classes because I had already done so at Ohio State University. Unfortunately, my dreams of being KDC's drummer crumbled during this time because there was inner turmoil amongst the band and they decided to call it quits. This all happened after I had been accepted into MI and made the decision to move out west.

I finished things up at school in NYC and passed the course and was even offered a job as a "live-in" raw food chef for a lawyer and her daughter in Manhattan but declined because of my stronger drive to be a musician. Who knew there was work out there for someone with such niche interests as mine? I was proven wrong even though I declined the job offer. Finally I was on a path that really made sense to me! It actually felt like the right decision for the first time and not something I was settling on out of fear.

In order to save money, I moved back to Columbus for six months and helped with the opening of a new vegan restaurant with my former head chef. Upon returning, he hired me on as his assistant chef, even though I would only be in town for six months. That was a lot of fun for me. During that time, I just practiced the drums a lot, worked hard, saved money and got to cook some really fancy dishes at the new restaurant. He let me come up with some of my own specials too, which was really exciting for me. I'll always look back fondly at that experience. Cooking may not have been what I'd pursue full-time but I sure do have fun doing it and continue to gain knowledge in the field as life moves forward.

Time moved forward and eventually I made it out to California to pursue my big dreams as a musician and to finish my degree at Musician's Institute.

Chapter 2
Novice Vegan

During the first couple of years living in Los Angeles, I pretty much operated in a routine way. I practiced my drums, went to school and lacked a social life. I didn't join any bands or try to start anything because all that I wanted to do was to get better. I figured if I simplified my life, it would be easier to get to a level of playing that would allow for me to be ready to play with whoever I wanted to in the future. I remained vegan during this time but didn't try to find work in vegan restaurants or up my home cooking game much by experimenting in my kitchen. I did become a teacher's assistant at MI, which helped me financially a little bit but I had left the professional cooking arena.

While at MI, I stuck to a lot of "poor-man's" vegan dishes. I made beans with rice, soups, pasta and I consumed a few convenience foods such as veggie burgers and veggie hot dogs. I still hadn't quite looked at the vegan lifestyle in terms of health and I drifted from the raw lifestyle because I had a difficult time not eating all of the time and feeling sluggish. My new approach was that of a "junk food vegan." I had a deep fryer at the time and I sure had a great time using that. I made my own batter dipped tofu with BBQ sauce, french fries, hush puppies and just about any other deep fried vegan concoction that I could come up with. I think my early-20's body miraculously was able to handle the stress that I am sure it was causing my liver, heart and kidneys. I wouldn't recommend anyone to try this though. The comedown from the dopamine rush I got from eating this drug-like food caused a lot of difficulty leaving my couch. There was too much fat, sugar and salt in the food I was eating.

I was always pretty skinny on the vegan diet too. I may have been skinny eating meat as well. Who knows? My brother still ate meat and we both had a similar build. I think I just lucked out with having a fast metabolism and good genetics because with the amount of fat that I was consuming, I'm sure it could have been detrimental to my weight and overall health. I wasn't very active either unless you count practicing the drums. That was something that eventually changed.

During my time in school, around the final year, my love for industrial and goth music grew. Through a buddy, I had the opportunity to audition for Meg Lee Chin of Pigface. I was extremely nervous about auditioning, so I practiced the two songs that I had to learn over and over for hours. I had stars in my eyes because I saw her perform with Pigface at a large venue on the Sunset Strip. I thought that if I get the gig, I'll be out there touring the world, playing venues like that every night. This would be way bigger than anything I had done up to that point. I toured a lot during my teenage years but as I mentioned earlier, it was house parties, recreational centers, dive bars and in some cases "laundry mat bars." I think this was something unique to Ohio, where you can wash your clothes while sipping on beer and watching a band perform.

When I arrived at the rehearsal spot where Meg and her band mates were warming up, I shielded my nervous feelings and tried not to say too much and just let the music do the talking. Meg said, "You look cool, so I hope this all works out." That made me relax a little but made me really zero in on the playing which was where I was a bit more anxious. We played about eight bars of the first song and she was like, can you do it again but with a bit more of a "dub-reggae" feel to it? What did that even mean? This was an industrial rock tune and I knew what reggae was but not dub-reggae, so I proceeded to play the song again with a lot of emotion but the way I practiced it and heard it on the album. She stopped me again and said, "Hey man, sorry, this just isn't the right feel. This isn't going to work. Thanks for coming out." That was a humbling moment. I slowly packed up my drums and proceeded to my car. Her guitarist followed me out there with some of my gear. His name was Steven and he was the singer of another industrial band that I was a big fan of called "Hate Dept." As we made it to my car, he said, "Hey man, she may not have liked what you did, but I liked it. Can you play some keyboards as well? I need a drummer who can play some keys for a Hate Dept. tour coming up because my normal guy was in an automobile accident and I'm unsure if he'll recover in time." Talk about turning a bad situation into a good one! I was honored even though I still felt horrible about the rejection that I just got.

I took Steven up on the offer and he became not only a leader of mine with Hate Dept., but also a mentor in a lot of ways when it came to doing my own music. He took me on my first tour out in California with Hate Dept. and Hanzel Und Gretyl. He also helped me to mix and master my first album; called Mankind is Obsolete, that I put out on my own with my college girlfriend. Steven taught me a lot about production and recording and I've always looked up to him. Down the line he also went vegan and works with rescue dogs with his wife "Michelle" who was also in Pigface with him. Touring with Hate Dept. was where I started to lay down the foundations of touring as a vegan.

In the beginning, vegan or not, I had to make things work on a shoestring budget. Most musicians can probably identify with this.   I'm talking about surviving on $5 to $10 per day. Most people when travelling will drop a lot of weight from being in a calorie deficit on this kind of income if it isn't spent properly, so I had to start wising up, fast. Lack of funds and my alternative lifestyle led me to start thinking about healthy choices. Back when I had a job working at a restaurant and living in a cheap "$200 per month" apartment in Columbus, I was able to eat out more and I enjoyed vegan cheeseless pizzas, burritos from the local Mexican restaurant that didn't use lard in the beans, Ethiopian and Indian cuisine and other seemingly luxurious choices. All of that changed. If I was going to survive on a meager income, I needed to start thinking of the healthiest choices for the least amount of money. Even as times got better for me, I still lock into this way of thinking when on tour. Also, eating the way I do now and on tour is actually a lot less expensive than eating the standard American diet or even a processed vegan diet filled with meat analogues and faux cheese.

This newly found predicament of mine was a milestone in my quest for not only being vegan for the animals, but also being vegan for my health and trying to find out how to truly be healthy with this diet.

When we were out on this tour, I really had to fend for myself. There wasn't catering at the shows and I don't think we ever got buy-outs either. A lot of times when a tour is booked, some of the guarantee for what a band will make is given out in the form of a buy-out. Everyone within the touring group and crew will get usually around $10-$20 to pay for food or any basic needs that the individual may have during that day. This is given out or sometimes the venue will provide a meal instead. If you are on a really low budget tour or if you are a support band, this may not be factored in. You may have to draw from the actual income you make per show or in the case of my own bands, draw from your personal savings. In that case, you really have to tighten the belt because the money you make may need to go towards your rent back home, bills, pet food, money you owe your friend, etc... Most musicians I know start off in this humble way where they are pretty much paying out of their pocket to play shows. Going on tour ends up costing them money instead of providing money. Luckily, I started off breaking even in most cases where the tour paid for itself. I didn't walk home with money but I didn't really lose money either.

I never started off in music making much money. As a result, I got used to being thrifty immediately, so that I could take on any tour that came my way. I thought that you'd have to be in Metallica to really make a living doing music. I just assumed everyone was poor doing this, especially after meeting some former rock gods out in Los Angeles during my early years. I met people living in a crappy Hollywood apartment with their gold records hung up on the wall selling off their personal items for cash, if that says something. I also recall that as I was touring in underground scenes, I was playing some of the same size venues I remember growing up and seeing my heroes play in, and also in front of the same small crowds. If I wasn't making hardly enough money, I'm sure they were not either. The times were changing. This wasn't the 80's anymore where if you saw someone on MTV, he or she must have a sick house and an Italian sports car. I certainly ran across this fantasy. It exists but a vast amount of people I'd see gracing the best stages around the world did so making a humble living unless they had other sources of income or other factors that I have yet to discover.

But I digress. So off we go, the first food stop on this Hate Dept. tour was Taco Bell. I will say this now. I am not and will probably never be a fan of fast food restaurants for a number of reasons. The food is generally some of the more unhealthy choices available and usually the company ethics and business practices are shady and corrupt to say the least. All that being said, Taco Bell does have vegan options. I do support them when it is necessary. If you are touring in this manner, they are an affordable option to consider. Back when I was eating at such a place, they had this $0.99 menu where you could order "Fresco Style" bean burritos. This is a sensible choice if you are on a budget and touring, and you can have the comforts of a warm meal that just so happens to be vegan. Having a cooked meal, even if it is a fast food one does a lot to boost one's spirits. I recommend it at least once a day while traveling. Things can be done in a healthier manner, which I'll dive into later, but I think getting one solid meal like this will help your morale.

In the "Fresco Style" bean burrito, you're getting beans, tomatoes, onions, cilantro and a red sauce. I'm sure there is some unhealthy fat in the form of hydrogenated soy bean oil and sodium in there but as a young buck on the road, my body didn't seem to reject this food too much. There are some other cheap places that also have vegan items like Del Taco. I believe you can still get their bean and cheese burrito, minus the cheese for $0.99 as well and the beans taste a lot better in my opinion. So this is fast food, and there are certainly quite a few choices out there that are vegan in this realm. Some places have even healthier options such as Chipotle or Veggie Grill but these chains are not as common as the above mentioned. Again, I find fast food to not be the healthiest of choices, but I certainly ate this way while on tour in the beginning. It is good to know that the option exists especially when you don't have many options available.

This brings me to the point of preparation. It is so important to be prepared for things like this. I learned the hard way, like most people probably do where you end up having to spend money unnecessarily on inferior quality food because you are on the road at 2am in a state like Wyoming and your choices are a truck stop or starve until the next 24 hour Wal-Mart shows up on your route. I'll write more about being prepared soon, but this gives you a glimpse into some of the roadblocks you may incur while touring as a vegan, or just touring in general. We're all usually in a constant search for an affordable meal in a remote location during an hour when most businesses are closed.

We live in the internet age now, where it is much easier to find exactly what one needs almost instantaneously, so having some of the same struggles I had may not apply much to anyone who is Google savvy. Look online and see what vegan fast food is available. It is always good to know before you embark on a tour. Find the chains that offer vegan options and try to get your group to stop at those restaurants. If there is something for everyone to eat, then everybody wins. I do sometimes get to tour with all vegan groups or vegan conscious groups, but that certainly isn't the norm. I'm typically the odd man out as far as food lifestyle goes. So on tours like I had with Hate Dept., I recall myself filling up on those cheap burritos and taking advantage of the complimentary brunch buffets at places like Super 8 Motels. These are great spots. They are generally very affordable compared to most other hotels and they offer free breakfast as well that usually includes things like oatmeal, cereal, juice, fresh fruit and coffee. I would load up on the oatmeal and sometimes just add apple juice to my cereal. Try it! It isn't bad. I'd also partake in the coffee and fresh fruit. Lastly, when looking online, try sites like Happy Cow. They even have a cell phone application that locates all vegan restaurants, grocery stores, or places with vegan options. I've used it many times and it works globally. You'll find vegan options in the most unlikely places! Always remember how simple it is just to grab a few things such as fruit, vegetables and nuts at a grocery store. Don't underestimate the power and ease of picking up these items that will help keep your chances of getting sick on the road to a minimum. Every grocery store carries these and if you're in a pinch, even gas stations carry a small amount of fruit. It is usually an unripe banana or an apple, but the options are there.

Some of what I did back then I still do now, but I continue to refine things as well as I get a better grip on understanding human nutrition. While on this tour, we would see a grocery store now and then and I'd try to grab a few things that were not perishable but still affordable. Rolled oats, peanuts and raisins are your saving grace. I made a combination of this on multiple tours and still eat this today even when I'm not on tour, with some small variations. I typically use fresh fruit like bananas and/or blueberries and I sprinkle ground up flax seed or walnuts on my oatmeal. Whether it's my home version or tour version, it is super cheap and as far as I know, it's a very healthy choice packed with fiber, vitamins, and other important nutrients which will give you a solid boost of energy for when you will perform later. All you need to do is have a bowl and spoon on hand, and getting hot water is easy. When you stop at a gas station, just get boiling water from the coffee machine for free! I usually ask even though it's just water because I assume that the cashier thinks I look shady walking in there in all black, usually with stage make-up still on my face. So by asking about the water with a smile, I figure I won't look like I'm stealing coffee.

In addition to oats, I would also typically get something perishable that I could munch on right away to help create some balance in my starch centered diet. It is common to see me get a head of kale, celery or carrots and start chowing down on that immediately as I hop back into the van. It is important to get some vegetables in your diet and when you are sitting in a van for hours waiting to get to the next town, you have all the time in the world to chew up kale so there are no excuses. It may seem a bit adventurous to some, but having this dense nutrient powerhouse food as part of a daily eating routine will pay off in your general health. Kale is packed with minerals, B vitamins, fiber and protein. If kale is too much for you to bear, start with carrots and celery. Just get some raw vegetables in the mix whenever you can. You'll want this in your diet so that you can have regular bowel movements. Yes, I said it. This is very important to good health. You should have at least one but as many as three bowel movements per day. Each meal you eat should be so loaded with fiber that you remain "regular." Ok, enough on that.

If I break things down a bit, you could get by doing this for under $10 in a day if you have to rely totally on yourself to take care of your food. If you were ever as poor as me, I could probably get it down even further when I go into more ways of approaching this. Three bean burritos at a fast food joint will set you back about $3.50 after tax. A head of kale is $1-$1.50. A box of instant oats will be about $1-$3 depending on the size of the box and where you purchase it, and keeping a box of raisins and peanuts around will add maybe a dollar or two depending on how much you eat in a day. Eat a solid breakfast when you have it available at some of those motels and bring an apple or two from the breakfast bar for the road. Do not go hungry! As much as quality of food matters, when traveling, we all have to bend a bit. Try not to bend on the quantity, as long as you are eating whole, natural, plant food. If you choose the right healthy foods, it is difficult to overdo it. Make sure you have sufficient calories during the day because you'll need that to function properly and to put on an energetic performance. I have not sufficiently fed myself enough on multiple occasions and it has had a negative effect on my ability to perform. Treat yourself as best as you can. Make sure you have a few of those staples around at all times. If you are dirt poor, be sure to at least have plenty of oats around as a foundation that is easy to prepare when travelling. From there just build upon the diet however you can.

It wasn't too bad the first couple of times on the road. I certainly went hungry occasionally and blew larger amounts of money at gas stations getting inferior quality peanut butter with "hydrogenated soy bean oil and sugar" and white bread. Again, I wasn't really thinking in the same way I am now, but I thought this was a manageable way to get by. Certainly the diet may seem to be a bit boring to some and eventually you may want to add some variety. Or you may have more lofty goals as I started to have later on when it came to health and the vegan diet.

I want to touch on why "hydrogenated vegetable oils" are so bad for you. First of all, vegetable oil is bad for you and the environment. The way vegetable oil is made involves high heat (500°F-1000°F) to a seed or nut which causes oxidation and makes the product rancid by the time you get it. It then goes through a process using petroleum solvents to extract the oil. After that, it is heated further with an acid solution added to help separate any waxy solids. Finally, it is treated with more chemicals to improve the color and smell. It has been proven to damage the lining of your endothelial cells in your heart and also cause atherosclerotic lesions. Another name for this kind of fat is "trans-fat." Trans-fat acts in a similar way to the fat found in animal products. It is to be noted that trans-fat naturally occurs in animal fat as well, so when we consume animal foods, we consume trans-fat.

The National Academy of Science has concluded that the only safe amount of trans-fat in one's diet is zero because any intake of trans-fat increases the chances of a person to develop coronary heart disease.[1] According to present studies in the British Journal of Medicine, any trans-fat intake, irrespective of source, increases cardiovascular disease "CVD" risk. So any hydrogenated oil or fat that comes from an animal protein source increases our risk of CVD.[2]

To find out more, check out the famous study that was published in The Journal of The American Medical Association by Dr. David H. Blankenhorn. He did a study where 82 heart patients were put on two different diets. One group continued with their high fat, high animal foods diet and the other limited their animal foods to no more than one egg a week or 6 ounces of fish. Also, the limited animal foods group had to include no added fats in the form of butter and oils. Guess who had more arterial plaque at the end of the study? The group with the oil and animal proteins![3] Don't let anyone fool you. Adding any sort of oil to your diet can be detrimental to your health. It is a processed food and offers next to no nutritional

---

[1] "NAS Panel: Only Safe Intake of Trans Fat Is Zero." *Center for Science in the Public Interest*, cspinet.org/new/200207101.html. Accessed 08/09/2017
[2] "Trans Fatty Acids and Cardiovascular Disease — NEJM." *New England Journal of Medicine*, www.nejm.org/doi/full/10.1056/NEJMra054035. Accessed 08/09/2017
[3] "Heart Study Finds Need to Cut Overall Fat in Diet." *The New York Times*, The New York Times, 23 Mar. 1990, www.nytimes.com/1990/03/24/us/heart-study-finds-need-to-cut-overall-fat-in-diet.html. Accessed

value. It is pure fat without any fiber and maybe only a hint of Vitamin E. It is also the most calorie dense food item on the planet and should be avoided especially by those struggling with obesity. It is easy to take down a tablespoon of olive oil and add 119 empty calories instantly. Avoid it by staying clear of processed foods, which typically contain sizeable amounts of oil and by not cooking with oil. There are plenty of ways to cook without added fat. I'll get into that shortly.

There is plenty of other evidence out there that oil is bad for humans. Type 2 diabetics or people looking to control their weight and for optimal health should remove oil from their diet. Standard vegetable oil is bad but hydrogenated oil is a whole other level of toxic to the body. Take all of those steps and add hydrogen molecules to the soybean oil so that it becomes solid at room temperature and it transforms a polyunsaturated fat into a saturated fat, which is horrible for heart health. This sort of fat thickens up your blood and makes your heart work on overtime trying to get blood through your system. It also raises your bad cholesterol, which is another reason why plaque then builds up on your arterial walls. Stay away from these fats at all costs. I found them in the common brands of peanut butter but you'll see them a lot in dessert foods and candy bars as well. There is no denying how horrible trans-fat and saturated fat is. Mainstream media has even jumped on board in the last few years and there has been a ban of trans-fats in eateries in New York City. By 2018, there should be a nationwide ban. This is all an improvement to our health but we still haven't tackled the problems of animal fat and vegetable oils such as olive, soy, corn and coconut, in regards to human health.

In the last 20 years or so we've been bombarded with how good some oils are for us, such as olive oil. These are based on short-term studies done by Scott M. Grundy, which showed some advantages for substituting olive oil for other oils when cooking, but longer-term studies on oil "of all sorts" have come up with unfavorable data regarding the use of oil. There is a wealth of information out there and I could go on about it but I highly recommend everyone to check out the number of articles, scientific journals and books out there on the subject. Check out any books by Dr. Greger, Dr. McDougall, Dr. Alan Goldhamer, Dr. Michael Klaper, or Dr. Esselstyn for more research information regarding harm of consuming oil. There are plenty of speeches from these esteemed doctors that can be found online for free as well, if you do a search on Google.

When touring and when at home, a simple approach is taken when it comes to eating. This approach is to eat only whole, unprocessed, plant foods. The meals I eat are generally pretty simple and I rotate between a few things each week. Some people need a lot of variety when it comes to what they eat, but I prefer simplicity, mostly out of convenience. For breakfast, it's almost always oatmeal with fruit. Dinner and lunch tend to be the same thing. I make large pots of soup, beans, cooked whole grains or roots, steamed greens and sometimes have salads in the summer time. I just pull from these prepared dishes and eat that throughout the day. I carry containers of these foods with me to my drum studio, and anywhere else I may need to be during the day. If I had more time, I'd orchestrate more entree possibilities and add a bit more variety, but what I do works for me.

Chapter 3
Getting Derailed

With a few tours under my belt and an ever-growing interest in health, I started to have some fears about the path I had been taking for these past few years. I was in my mid-twenties and the internet had been exploding as a means to gather information quickly. I was feeling weak and I didn't know why. I couldn't tell if it was the rigorous schedule that I had of balancing school, touring, practicing and writing music with bands, or lack of sleep because of stress and anxiety. I was also still dealing with a lot of issues from my father's suicide and how much my childhood affected me. I was in and out of therapy at that time due to either having health insurance or not having it. A lot was happening with me and I really wanted solutions so that I could go forth with my goals in life without so much chaos.

I decided that I would start exercising a bit. I had brought all of my old DVDs and vhs cassettes with me when I moved to Los Angeles. In the pile, I found one of my father's work out videos from the early 80's from former Mr. Olympia Franco Columbu. It was a basic strength and conditioning video that didn't involve much in the way of gear and it was designed for someone with not much fitness experience. One could perform all of the exercises with just a couple of dumbbells and it only took about 25 minutes to get through it. It is what gym enthusiasts would call a "circuit train." A circuit train is great for someone like me or others on the go because it combines a bit of cardiovascular exercise with strength building. Because you go through all of the major muscle groups in one work-out without much rest between sets, the heart rate remains elevated. I still draw from it today and I think this simple video has been the foundation of my exercise routine for the past 13 years. I find it to be the most pleasurable way to exercise at the gym and you can vary up the exercises for each muscle group too. One can also do circuit training to mix it up between days. I'll usually focus on upper body one day and the next will be lower body plus abdominal exercises. I'll repeat this 5-6 days per week. If you have loftier goals such as being a body builder, I wouldn't recommend this style of strength training. But for general strength and fitness, I find it to be the most efficient use of my time and effective in keeping my body in shape.

When I was first discovering fitness, I would also go running for about 15 minutes per day. There were these stairs near my apartment that went up a hill that was maybe 3 flights high. I would go up and down that a few times so that I was warmed-up and then I'd work out to the video after. It did help my energy levels to some degree, but I noticed that I was still tired and I couldn't figure out why. I was convinced that it had something to do with my diet. I started looking up the vegan diet online and tried to check a number of sources with professional opinions. I came across some of the pitfalls that researchers had discovered about the diet. One of the pitfalls was getting enough Vitamin B-12.

I didn't really know much about the vitamin at the time: which foods provided it, what happens if you become deficient in it, and so on. I just knew that it didn't come from plant sources and could only be obtained naturally through animal sources. This deeply disturbed me because it made it seem like my diet was flawed somehow. One can even find articles in popular health and fitness magazines that will still bring up this flaw when it comes to the vegan diet. I searched endlessly for reliable sources of vitamin B-12 in the plant world and was met with a lot of conflicting literature. Some sources would say it is available in spirulina (blue-green algae), nutritional yeast (brewer's yeast), sea vegetables or even unwashed vegetables. Other sources would claim that these were unreliable sources and that the only way for vegans to get this nutrient was through supplementation. Not only that, the type of supplementation was also up for debate as far as how well the human body could absorb the various forms out there.

Like cow's milk or other animal foods, a lot of vegan, processed products are supplemented with nutrients that are either stripped away during the refining process or are commonly a challenge for humans to obtain due to modern agricultural practices. This is why you'll see cereal or non-dairy milks supplemented with vitamins like B-12. Because of the nature of the vitamin, I have seen that this may not be a reliable way to absorb B-12, so other sources will say to get it sublingually through a pill that melts under your tongue or through vitamin B-12 shots that you would get through your doctor or at a health clinic.

I'll go more into general vegan health in the upcoming chapters, but this information about vitamin B-12 put the scare in me about what I was doing to a point that I rationalized being a pesco-vegetarian (fish, dairy and egg consuming vegetarian) for about a year and some change. I somehow justified that eating fish, eggs and dairy wasn't so bad and that I would finally get this nutrient that I needed. I can tell you that I really hated this phase of my life, though. I rationalized my change by feeling ok with eating an animal that wasn't a mammal like myself. I figured fish don't necessarily get enslaved and that they can swim free until they get caught for my consumption. It was weak logic, but I used it to make myself feel better. I also consumed dairy and eggs because I thought: "no animal had to die for this," which ultimately isn't true. In farming situations, cows and chickens that are bred for their eggs and milk are slaughtered for meat as soon as they hit a certain age, so by supporting the egg and dairy industry, you are still supporting the slaughter and enslavement of animals. I was in a lot of denial in order to make these new dietary tweaks, but I was supposedly getting the nutrient now. Even still, I hadn't checked my blood levels to see where I was at, so there is no telling if this was helping my health or hurting it. It also didn't really make me feel much better. I still had some weak feelings that may have just had to do with stress, little sleep, and taking on too much work. It was important to check the basics though. We all need good sleep, exercise, healthy food and low stress in order to achieve our maximum potential of positive health.

Even though I would maintain this modified vegetarian diet for a brief period, it did make touring easier at the time because my options grew. I could easily just tell promoters to pick up a cheese pizza instead of figuring out if there was a vegan restaurant nearby or getting my order confused with somebody because they don't really understand what a vegetarian is, let alone a vegan. I remember also eating a lot of canned tuna while on tour during this time because of its ease of storage and low price.

Eventually, I made my way out of this mode of thinking because I started noticing examples of long-term vegans who maintained some great health. There were also a lot more people in the medical and nutritional science community embracing the diet than there had been before and they were all gathering online in forums on various web pages. I remember how amazing it felt when I ditched the pesco-vegetarian lifestyle and went back to being vegan again. It even inspired me to go out there and prove that one can not only get by on this lifestyle but thrive and be a beacon of health, and possibly inspire others to try this out if they were ever considering it.

I became heavily into fitness at this point and really wanted to prove that I could have a ripped physique and do it all while being vegan. I thought that, I would never have to explain my diet again if I broke the stereotypes of vegans being these anemic weaklings. That was the idea that I thought people had, especially towards male vegans. Not knowing the future, I didn't realize that there would be so many examples of men that defy the stereotype of the hippy who lives off of granola, with zero physical strength. Today, I no longer feel the need to take things to the level that I did in my late twenties. I simply seek a healthy level of fitness that will give me the endurance to practice and perform the drums for hours.

I'm a pretty lean guy naturally and so are most of the men on my mother's side of the family. I never met or saw many family members from my father's side but my mom and her brothers and parents were all bean poles for a large portion of their lives. Some are still that way today. My brother is the same. He is about 6 ½ years older than me, eats meat and is still very lean. I think we have good genetics in that sense but I do see the men in my family who all follow the standard American diet starting to gain some excess weight. I don't know that they are as physically active anymore though, so that may explain some of the weight gain. Some of my favorite plant-based leaders are constantly explaining to their masses "you can't outrun a bad diet." I really believe that this is true. Exercise will thwart off some of the problems of a bad diet, and may keep your weight at a healthier level than if you were to not exercise at all, but it certainly won't provide you with optimal health.

So in my late twenties, I took my fitness to a whole other level. Part of this was to never have to explain my diet to anyone, because when you do something different, it typically comes with a mixture of scrutiny and amazement. I had a tendency to hold on to the scrutiny though. I wanted my diet to speak for itself. I thought to myself "how cool will it be, to be this lean and strong looking guy, who only eats plants?" My results would speak for themselves and I would be helping the imprisoned farm animals and promoting a lifestyle that I believe strongly in while also promoting good positive health. And let me tell you, it worked! It worked a few years back and with more years adding onto my life now, it has only strengthened my case for living this way.

The life of the aspiring musician is not an easy one, especially if you start focusing on your instrument later in life. During this "born-again" vegan era, I was living out of my drum studio and had a membership with the local gym, mainly to shower but I was also getting the opportunity to work out as well and lift heavy weights. The results happened quickly for me, and I gained muscle fast until I hit a plateau at 5'11" and 170 pounds. That may not sound like a weight-lifting beast, especially in the world of mass-steroid use, but for my frame, this was quite a change and a change that my peers noticed.

I was still young in my thoughts and this muscled physique brought me the confidence that I desired to spread awareness of the vegan lifestyle and smash any myths that any skeptics would have. I did notice a change when people would ask me about my diet and I simply would say that I don't eat animal products. I would get more of the amazed reaction instead of the scrutinizing reaction that I once had as a younger and scrawnier vegan. Mission accomplished!

The approach of leading by example fit better with my personality. When someone believes strongly in something, there are a number of different ways they can approach awareness of it. I've met people that approach veganism in a more radical way and they certainly have had an impact. There is a part of me that really admires this "no fucks given" attitude that these people have when it comes to their approach to the cause. Through my journey, I have felt the best way for me to approach this has been through a positive example. I want people to see me and think, "This guy looks good and healthy for his age. Maybe there is something to his lifestyle." At the time of writing this, I am 38 years old! I have years of experience, years of trial and error that I have experimented with when it comes to approaching veganism. I can attest that I feel better than ever physically and mentally, and I hope to enjoy many more years of positive health. I hope that my example and my experiences will inspire others who view our animal agriculture industry as despicable to give whole food, plant-based eating a try for the animals, our environment, and for our health.

I've created sort of a mission statement for myself and it has kept me on track for a while. I think that in order to sway more minds over to eating this way, I need to be well informed scientifically and in good shape physically. With that, I'll be able to reach people in a positive way about this and hopefully, more people will want to put an end to the animal enslavement industry and also look to veganism as a way of being healthy too.

Chapter 4
Vegan Health

As time moved forward from my late twenties until now, I maintained this vegan lifestyle and continued to educate myself on it. I refined my eating habits to maximize the energy I could have during a day. My job as a drummer is physical and requires a lot of focus that burns up a lot of fuel. So more now than ever, being healthy has been a primary focus of mine. I'm also not as young and resilient to poor social and nutritional choices anymore. I was once straight-edge, meaning "drug free" in the hard-core scene, but in my mid-twenties I started to drink beer occasionally and I even tried a couple of recreational drugs. Luckily, my drug use was just experimental and brief. I'm happy that I came out of that phase unscathed and with no desire to further my experimenting. Beer on the other hand is something that I still enjoy. I know it may not be the best thing for me, (though I am sure I can find enough scientific data that says it is ok for me in moderation,) but from the majority of the research that I have come across on the subject as well as my own experimenting goes, I know that it isn't the wisest of beverage choices. I can handle it in small doses on occasion and it seems to be fine with my system when I do so. That being said, I hope to have no more hangovers from crazy binge drinking moments like I had in my late 20's. Luckily my binge drinking moments are scarce, if not extinct these days. I hope to have little to no more of those in my life. Maybe one day, I will give it up entirely, but for now, I will enjoy the occasional beer or two during a social outing a few times per year. On a side note, it is good to know which beers and wines are actually vegan. This was something that I had no idea about for a long time. There are a few alcoholic beverages that use fish bladder or egg whites in the filtration process. Many standard American domestic beers happen to be vegan as are a lot of micro brews, but it is always good to check. A simple google.com search will give you the answers you need. I think PETA has information on which beers are vegan as well.

Over the years, I read a number of excellent books on the subject of health and nutrition and I highly recommend the readers to check some of these out if you want to dive deeper into human health and plant based diets. They have certainly helped me tie up a lot of loose ends with my diet and it is great to know that there is a lot of science that backs up my food choices. Notable people and their books to check out in the vegan nutrition world are: Dr. Greger "How Not To Die," Caldwell B. Esselstyn Jr. "Prevent and Reverse Heart Disease," Dr. John A. McDougall "The Starch Solution," Dr. Neal Barnard's "Program for Reversing Diabetes," Dr. Douglas J. Lisle and Dr. Alan Goldhamer "The Pleasure Trap: Mastering the Hidden Forces that Undermines Health & Happiness" and Dr. T Colin Campbell "The China Study." Pretty much all of these authors wouldn't consider the diet that they promote as vegan per se, but they in fact, are. They just so happen to be vegan with a focus on promoting healthy living. There are certainly unhealthy ways to approach this diet. There are vegan pastries, fried foods, and processed foods that all may be void of animal products, but over time a diet that incorporates too much of these foods can be detrimental to one's health and well-being. I find them good only for rare social moments, transitional phases from the Standard American Diet over to a vegan diet and if you are simply starving with nothing else to eat.

I'd like to now start with the basics of health and nutrition so that I can later on discuss how to tour or travel as a vegan in the healthiest possible way. If you are reading this, chances are you are already health conscious or vegan and struggling to find some tips on how to make things easier as you travel. I am going to outline what I believe are the fundamentals of a healthy vegan diet. If you want to further your education, by all means, check out any of the great books that I listed above. Also, many of those doctors that I mention above have great online resources for free! Dr. McDougall and Dr. Greger both have fantastic websites with a wealth of science-based information. In the books, videos and websites, you'll find scientific journals, large-scale epidemiological studies on human nutrition, "The China Study," and plenty of arguments for a whole foods, plant-based, vegan diet that is free of refined sugar, little or no added salt and no vegetable oil.

Let's begin by examining what the healthiest vegan diet is. It is my belief based on the research I have done, as well as my own experimenting, that the healthiest diet is a whole foods, plant-based, one. Let's start off by breaking down the meaning of this. A whole foods diet means eating a single ingredient food in its entirety and unprocessed form. For example, eating brown rice as opposed to white rice, which is a processed form of brown rice. White rice no longer contains the hull and bran that it once did and has lost some of its vitamins, minerals and fiber that were contained in the removed parts. When you refine a food such as rice, it can create nutritional imbalances. It can also be a contributing factor to overeating. The body is very intelligent. When we eat fragmented foods, our body gets confused and we run the risk of eating too much as our bodies may not feel satiated due to the lack of fiber or other parts that were missing from the original food. We also may not be getting all of the nutrients from the original food when we eat it in a processed form. Over time, this can lead to deficiencies and other health issues. From personal experience, I can easily eat four to five times the recommended serving of calorically dense cookies or some other manufactured product and still not feel satiated. It is possible to consume 1000 calories in a sitting without the stretch receptors in my stomach noticing that I'm consuming this much. I may feel exhausted afterwards but I can binge eat on these types of foods because they lack the fiber and a lot of the vitamins and minerals that the whole components of each ingredient once had. Not to mention, these fragmented and processed foods are often high in salt, sugar and fat and are so rich that they cause a heroin like high by spiking dopamine "feel-good neurotransmitter" levels in the brain. It is the main reason we crave these ultra sensational foods when we're hungry because they are so calorie dense and cause us to release large volumes of dopamine. Who hasn't gone through a whole bag of potato chips or a box of cookies in one sitting? I think most of us have been guilty of this at least a few times. It's another reason why common foods that are served at a brunch buffet, even a vegan one, can make us all tired at the end because our bodies are working overtime to process all of the refined products we just stuffed ourselves with. Think about how you feel when you eat a meal of pancakes with syrup, hash brown potatoes dripping in vegetable oil and white bread toast with jelly. If we ate this for breakfast, most of us would be searching for a bed to sleep on shortly after. Refined foods like this, which are lacking in fiber and high in fat, tend to give us a quick high followed by a crash.

This is part of the reason why foods like the potato get a bad reputation. A potato as a whole food is a fantastic part of the vegan diet but a lot of research on potatoes are done when they are in the form of french fries. They are usually stripped of the skin, which contains valuable fiber and nutrients, coated in vegetable oil and salt, and then fried at a high temperature. At this point, potatoes are no longer a healthy food.

Another example of a fragmented food would be corn oil versus whole corn. Corn oil or other vegetable oils generally go through heavy processing involving harmful solvents and high heat during the extraction. You are left with a product that is concentrated fat with little nutritional advantages and a lot potentially artery clogging disadvantages. When you consume corn in its whole foods form, you're getting the fiber, the vitamins and the macronutrients such as the fat, all in a harmonious way that the body is able to function more optimally on. For further information or to dive deeper into the science angle of this, I highly recommend checking out any of those books I mentioned. They are all packed with detailed information on the subject especially in the works of Dr. Caldwell Esselstyn or Dr. Neal Barnard. Fat is often the culprit for heart disease and Dr. Esselstyn explains the dangers of oil and teaches how to prevent and reverse heart disease through a whole food, plant-based diet that omits added vegetable oils[4].

So what does "plant-based" mean? Plant-based means simply to eat foods that are exclusively from the fruit and vegetable world, or "plant world." Plants provide everything that the human body needs in regards to nutrition. All of the vitamins and minerals you need for optimal health can be obtained through the consumption of plants. There isn't a single nutrient that needs to be obtained from an animal source and that includes Vitamin B12, which I wrote briefly about earlier and will go into more detail soon. Vitamin D may be the only other nutrient that is necessary on a plant-based diet but our bodies will synthesize it when exposed to a moderate amount of sunlight. It can only be a problem in certain northern countries where sunlight exposure is less during certain times of the year. That may be the only situation where Vitamin D could present a problem and a supplement should be considered during the winter months when sun exposure is less likely to happen.

So how do I do this? What foods do I eat? The good news is that the options are endless, especially if you understand some basic food preparation techniques, which everyone should learn how to do, regardless of what diet path they choose to follow. I think by now, most experts would all agree that even if animal products are consumed, that a whole foods diet is the optimal one for everyone on the planet. In order to eat this way, we need to prepare our food more often and rely less on restaurants and packaged foods. Most prepackaged food,

---

[4] Esselstyn, Caldwell. *Prevent and Reverse Heart Disease*. Avery, 2007.

vegan or not, tends to be highly processed, refined and usually containing a lot of unnecessary fat in the form of oil, as well as an abundance of refined sugar, salt, and chemical preservatives. If we want to be healthy, we should start with eating a whole foods diet. It doesn't have to be extremely complicated or expensive either. So don't fear having to be a master chef in order to pull this off. I'll show you ways you can do this with limited culinary skills and with limited finances, something that is often the case when not only living at home, but when touring as well. The glorious thing about eating this way is that it is not only helpful for your body, but often the wisest food choices are also the least expensive ones, contrary to popular opinion. People often think a vegan diet is expensive because they've been to places like Whole Foods Market that carry an abundance of vegan products and they spend a bit more than they would at your average grocery store. This is true, if you spend your time in the processed food sections. I stay away from those sections no matter what grocery store I am in. You only need to be in two sections, the produce section and the bulk foods section. Or, if there isn't a bulk foods section, the aisle that has beans, rice, legumes, and other grains, nuts and seeds. I just bought a fair amount of food at Whole Foods Market recently and it didn't cost more than $30. So you can shop there too and still find great items at a low cost. You don't have to buy expensive "super foods" or products that some health guru is trying to sell you online. You also don't have to load up on faux meat and cheese products that mimic the animal products we once ate before. Simplicity is the key. Don't ever let anyone tell you that eating this way is expensive. It is cheaper to make a pot of beans, rice and steamed kale than it is to buy a "value meal" at your favorite fast food place.

When dealing with a whole-food, plant-based diet, the ideal foods would also be organic and locally grown so that we don't add pesticides, fungicides and other potentially harmful chemicals that could be present in our food. Even if organic and locally sourced food isn't something that is in your budget or available where you live, making these other dietary tweaks will still help you tremendously when it comes to warding off common food-caused illnesses. Local produce is important because it isn't being shipped from the other half of the world where strawberries may be in season, so not only will you get fresher produce if you buy locally, it will also lower the carbon footprint by eliminating all of the travel that it took to get out of season berries.

If you can't afford organic, don't worry. Buy conventional over not eating more plants, and make the decision to cook a simple plant-based meal over eating out at an unhealthy restaurant. Be sure to wash your produce well and know that certain fruits with peels such as bananas or oranges will have less exposure to pesticides than say berries, which may have the largest amount of pesticides on them if conventionally grown.

Also, when you eat commercially grown produce, it has a lot less of a harmful impact pound for pound than animal products have. Animal foods accumulate a concentrated build-up of pesticides as well as hormones and antibiotics in their tissue over time, so you are getting more pesticides in you from a pound of conventional beef than a pound of conventional soy[5]. Choose organic whenever possible. If you are ambitious and have the means, start a garden where you are the master over your own food production. I have dreams of the day when I will have a piece of land to grow my own fruits and vegetables.

Here is what vegans eating a whole-foods, plant-based diet consume: In a nutshell, we eat grains, beans, legumes, seeds, nuts, tubers, roots, fruits and vegetables. That's it! You don't need to check labels. It is one ingredient in each item of food. Here is some brown rice. Here are some apples. Here is a bunch of kale. It's simple! I'll expand on this as we go, but if you are eating these things in their whole food form, you're on the right track.

When discussing nutrition, we tend to break things down into macronutrients and micronutrients and then discuss calories or "food energy units." It is a complex science but I will break things down just a bit in layman's terms.

The macronutrients are fat, protein and carbohydrates. Every bit of food that you consume has a combination of these three macronutrients in various ratios and it is important to find a balance in them when making your food choices. Most of the research (as well as personal experience that I have had) supports leaning towards a macronutrient ratio that favors the majority of our foods being high in carbohydrates and low in fat and protein. Some people even wrote books about this or

---

[5] *McDougall Newsletter - Cesspool,*
www.drmcdougall.com/misc/2004nl/040800pucesspool.htm.
Accessed 08/07/2017

have created blogs online regarding this concept, especially amongst vegans that do not cook their own food (raw food vegans). If you go and research these concepts you can learn more in the book 80/10/10 by Dr. Doug Graham. The idea is that we should aim to have 80% of our macronutrients to be in the form of carbohydrate, 10% in fat, and 10% in protein. This term gets tossed around a lot by not only raw foodists, but by other people that follow a whole-foods, plant-based diet. With the research out there, if one wants to lower their risk of a lot of food-related illness, it is best to shoot for a diet with this macronutrient ratio in mind.

I dabbled in the raw-vegan lifestyle a few times during my vegan path and saw some benefit to it, but I also found that it was very expensive. I needed to eat a high volume of food, even higher than now, more often during the day. I felt great doing so, but we all bend a little in order to assimilate into our modern lifestyles, so I would still incorporate some cooked food items at times. I still eat a large amount of raw fruit and vegetables, but the bulk of my calories come from cooked starches. This gives me a bit more sustained energy throughout the day and costs a lot less. My macronutrient ratio still reflects the 80/10/10 principal though. This way of looking at macronutrients has served me well as far as fueling me for my day goes. I view myself in the same way now as to when I was a swimmer, and swimmers always ate a lot of pasta or high carbohydrate dinners before a competition. Between riding my bike everywhere, playing the drums and going to the gym, I still exert the same amount of energy in a day that many professional endurance athletes do. When you look at their diets, they tend to focus heavily on starches and fruits as their main fuel sources. In other words, the diet is high in carbohydrates.

In my nutritional journey, I have come across additional anthropological research on human nutrition that suggests we have evolved to primarily consume cooked starches due to the high amounts of amylase, an enzyme that breaks down carbohydrates in our saliva glands. Also, anthropologists have discovered large amounts of plant and starch matter and the absence of animal foods in the dental calculus of Neanderthals in Spain. This suggests that we may have evolved to eat in a more plant-based way[6].

But haven't we evolved to eat meat because of us being primarily hunters and gatherers? This question comes up often and even though it is correct that at times we hunted and ate meat over thousands of years to survive, it wasn't always our primary source of food calories. We certainly did not eat as much meat as we consume today in industrialized societies. Meat or animals were harder to catch and would spoil a lot quicker due to lack of refrigeration or preservatives, so it wasn't consumed as the main part of most civilizations" meals. Starches (potatoes, rice, corn, etc.) could be kept easier and provided the bulk of our calories. World-renowned anthropologist Nathaniel Dominy from Dartmouth College has this to say: "A majority of calories for most hunter-gatherer societies came from plant foods, not animal-foods, thus humans might be more appropriately

---

[6] Davis, Nicola. "Neanderthal Dental Tartar Reveals Plant-Based Diet – and Drugs." *The Guardian*, Guardian News and Media, 8 Mar. 2017, www.theguardian.com/science/2017/mar/08/neanderthal-dental-tartar-reveals-plant-based-diet-and-drugs. Accessed 08/07/2017

described as 'starchivores.'"[7] If you look at most traditional societies around the globe, you'll find that the center of the diet is a cooked carbohydrate source. In Asia it's rice and to a lesser extent, sweet potatoes. In Peru, it's potatoes, in North and Central America it's corn, in ancient Egypt it is wheat, in Africa it's millet, in the Middle East it's barley and oats, in parts of Europe it's legumes and in Northern Europe it is rye. It is believed by some that before we discovered fire, we ate a diet primarily based around raw plant foods. There are some that believe we should still be eating this way today but due to conflicting research out there, I believe we evolved to eat cooked starches in addition to a diet containing a high volume of raw fruits and vegetables. Of course in the case of survival, we ate whatever we could. The ever-growing scientific research out there, it continues to support the idea that a whole-food, plant-based diet is the optimal way for humans to eat for the best overall health and to avoid and reverse some diet-related illnesses.

There are many health experts and nutritional gurus out there that promote this way of eating where the vast amount of calories need to come from high carbohydrate, raw fruits such as bananas, mangos, grapes, dates, etc. to achieve maximum health benefits. It is a common belief among raw-food vegans that we are the only animals that cook our food and that it is unnatural to do so. YouTube health gurus Durianrider and Freelee The Banana Girl also popularized the "Raw Till 4" lifestyle, which advocates eating a lot of raw, high carbohydrate fruit during the day but having a high-carb, low-fat, cooked

---

[7] *McDougall Newsletter: January 2012 - Excerpt from The Starch Solution*, www.drmcdougall.com/misc/2012nl/feb/excerpt.htm. Accessed 08/07/2017

meal at night. For example, one could eat bananas, mangos, and grapes during the day and baked potatoes and a large salad at night.

According to Dr. John McDougall, we humans evolved from a similar eating strategy. It was common for us to search for raw fruits and vegetables during the day, and to have one large, cooked, starch-based meal at night. This had a lot to do with the difficulty of making a fire but the vast amount of our caloric intake during the day came from that cooked starch meal at night. It is true that hunter/gatherer groups also ate meat but it wasn't nearly as available and consumed as often as humans eat it today. The bulk of their diet came from starchy roots, fruits and vegetables. Humans were trim eating this way back then and didn't experience some of the same food-related illnesses that humans experience today. These days, due to eating excessive amounts of animal products and processed foods, coupled with a sedentary lifestyle, we as a society are crippled with lifestyle-related diseases. If you look at a lot of traditional cultures that haven't been impacted by the Western diet, you'll see that they don't have heart disease, Type 2 Diabetes, and certain forms of cancer. They may have other issues due to poor water sources or lack of food, but it isn't the same illnesses that we get in America, where we experience nutritional excess coupled with a sedentary lifestyle and a reliance on pharmaceuticals for every ailment.

Evidence based on large epidemiological research such as T. Colin Campbell's "The China Study" suggest that focusing the diet on high carbohydrate, low fat and low protein foods is ideal for optimal health and nutrition. I'll explain why. In the study of people living on a diet centered mostly on rice and vegetables in rural China over decades, most diseases that afflict Western populations such as heart disease, diabetes, and various forms of diet-related cancer were absent[8]. People would live to a ripe age and only when groups would move to more industrialized parts of the world and adopt diets rich in animal protein, fat and refined carbohydrates, would they start to develop the same dietary diseases that are weakening the Western world. I highly recommend checking out that book. It is a real eye-opener and has helped me get closer to optimal health by understanding the traps we face with eating habits in modern, Western civilization.

Think about a lot of traditional societies and the foods that they eat. If you travel a lot and get the chance to experience different parts of the globe, you'll see that the focal point of many traditional diets is a high-carbohydrate, whole food or simply put, a starch. The groups of people that live the longest and healthiest lives had a focus on starch with the addition of fruits, vegetables and in some cases limited animal protein. These societies tended to be more agrarian and so physical activity was common throughout their days all the way up until their golden years. In our own backyard in America, we have the Seventh Day Adventists which are a group of Christians that follow a vegetarian diet, avoid caffeine and

---

[8] Campbell, T. Colin, and Thomas M. Campbell. *The China Study: the Most Comprehensive Study of Nutrition Ever Conducted and the Startling Implications for Diet, Weight Loss and Long-Term Health.* BenBella Books, Inc., 2016.

alcohol and their average life expectancy is 10 years above that of the average American[9].

The vegan diet that I see as best should focus heavily on high-carbohydrate, whole-foods: beans, rice, barley, corn, buckwheat, wheat, potatoes, sweet potatoes, millet, quinoa, etc. This should be what you eat to get the most energy. Every cell in our body runs on glucose, which is carbohydrate broken down to its simplest form. If the body can't find carbohydrate to break down, its secondary choice is fat. Fat is an important nutrient and there are a lot of people out there that take an opposing stance when it comes to diet and opt for a high fat, high protein, low carbohydrate diet where the body uses fat as its main source of energy. This concept was at one point popularized by the famous weight loss doctor, Dr. Atkins, and can be seen in other forms like the popular "Paleo diet." These diets have had some studies showing people losing weight short-term, but with all of the saturated fat in them in the form of bacon and butter, these people run a greater risk of heart disease, Type 2 Diabetes and stroke. Also, a lot of people have a hard time keeping up with this diet that avoids most carbohydrates and may run into problems of binging on unhealthy concentrated, processed, sugary products because their cells desperately need glucose. This sort of diet strategy can create a yo-yo effect and I don't recommend it.

---

[9] Gary E. Fraser, MB, ChB, PhD. "Ten Years of Life." *Archives of Internal Medicine*, American Medical Association, 9 July 2001, jamanetwork.com/journals/jamainternalmedicine/fullarticle/648593. Accessed 08/07/2017

There is a lot of debate regarding what is healthy and what isn't and it is a huge subject to tackle. My belief is that humans were designed and evolved to eat grains, tubers, roots, fruit and vegetables as their main sources of food based on the findings of T. Colin Campbell and Dr. Caldwell Essylstyn Jr. But let's face it, carbohydrates have had a bad reputation for years now as being the culprits of dietary disease such as diabetes and obesity. The problem is that in a lot of research that is done with common carbohydrate foods, it is done with refined carbohydrates such as white rice, bread with refined flour, and potatoes in the form of potato chips or french fries that are covered in refined oil. A whole potato with its skin attached, either baked or boiled is quite low in fat and doesn't cause insulin spikes in the same way it does if it loses its peel and is attached with oil or some other form of unhealthy fat. In addition, eating refined carbohydrates in conjunction with high fat foods causes Type 2 Diabetes. When the body consumes too much fat, we get Free Fatty Acids (FFA) in our blood stream that interfere with glucose metabolism. When you then consume refined carbohydrates (without their natural fiber) the pancreas, which secretes insulin to metabolize glucose, gets confused, not releasing the appropriate amount or none at all. After continual damage due to poor dietary choices, Type 2 Diabetes sets in[10].

When you come across one of these brief health advice articles in a magazine or online, you also have to check and see who is funding such research. Most big

---

[10] FACLM, Michael Greger M.D. "What Causes Insulin Resistance?" *NutritionFacts.org*, nutritionfacts.org/video/what-causes-insulin-resistance/. Accessed 08/07/2017

businesses want to continue having success, so if there is research that makes their product look bad, they find a way to present contradictory data, (even if its poorly tested or a simple case study) and blast it at the general public through commercial brainwashing. I couldn't get past my morning cartoons as a child without seeing milk commercials between every break and there is growing evidence that milk is harmful for human consumption. But hey, it has calcium in it, so we get bombarded with that single detail constantly because the human body does, in fact, need calcium. However, it fails to mention that our bodies thrive on more alkaline diets and milk is highly acid forming as are all animal foods. Therefore, milk will actually contribute to leaching calcium and other minerals from our bones and contribute to the formation of kidney stones.[11] Cow milk is also responsible for children developing too quickly during youth because of the amount of hormones in dairy products. The only milk we should be consuming is from our mothers during infancy. Lastly, how many people would go up to a cow right now and start sucking on her utters to drink her milk? Sound gross? We don't make the connection because we see milk in the form of ice cream, butter and cheese with a cartoon picture of a smiling cow on the front of the package. It becomes a product that often acts as a dopamine-raising drug, especially when coupled with refined sugars in the form of ice cream. Let's not forget the amount of saturated fat in dairy products that again, leads to the illnesses of the western world heart disease, Type-2 Diabetes, and certain types of cancer.

---

[11] *The McDougall Newsletter - When Friends Ask: "Why Don't You Drink Milk?,"* www.drmcdougall.com/misc/2007nl/mar/dairy.htm. Accessed 07/08/2017

The dairy industry is huge, though. (As are other large industries.) They'll fight tooth and nail to have their products looking good to the general public, even when there is a lot of science-based evidence that suggest their products cause harm to humans. But hey, it has calcium right?

High fat diets have also been proven to be dangerous and can be a contributing factor to heart disease and diabetes. On a personal note, most people that I have encountered who try to diet on high protein or high fat foods and avoid high carbohydrate foods, eventually binge on very unhealthy foods such as ice cream or cakes because they are starving themselves of the glucose that all of their cells need. This dieting tends to create a yo-yo effect with a lot of people. Their will power will keep them on the diet because it does in fact make you lose weight initially. But it is unsustainable in the long term, and can also lead to damaging your internal organs such as the kidneys and liver with all of the excess protein one needs to consume on these diets. If you don't believe me, look at what happened to Dr. Atkins and also look at the bodies of the people that tend to promote this lifestyle. Are they trim and have they been healthy looking long term, or ever? Remember all of the traditional societies who focus their diet on a starch. They tend to be trim and aren't plagued with the same dietary challenges that afflict the rich western world.

This leads me to the protein question. All vegans get this question at some point. Where do you get your protein? The idea that being vegan will make you protein deficient is a fallacy. If you are eating enough calories throughout the day, you'll get plenty of protein. I usually ask people if they know of anyone who suffers from a protein deficiency if confronted by this question and they can't name one. The only people with a protein deficiency are people who are starving to death, usually because of eating disorders or because of lack of ample portions of food in impoverished countries. The medical term for protein deficiency is "Kwashiorkor." If vegans had a protein deficiency, you'd be hearing this term more often. It is extremely uncommon for anyone. In the US we need to worry more about excessive protein issues rather than a lack of, so as long as you have had ample amounts of food during the day, you shouldn't worry about getting enough protein.

What is protein? What are good sources? Protein consists of long chains of amino acids and by eating enough plant foods to satisfy you, you'll be obtaining the amount of essential amino acids necessary for your body to repair itself or build muscle. This is why body builders stress eating tons of protein, because protein helps to rebuild muscle after it has broken down during a heavy weight training session. I assure you though, unless your goals are to be a body builder, which tends to be a potentially unhealthy goal because of the excess amounts of protein that the body must metabolize, and then worry about getting enough calories from whole plant foods and you'll be getting enough protein.

I've watched a lot of documentaries over the past couple of years and I've seen a few on professional athletes who have retired. They may have been a beacon of health and strength during their heyday, but often as they age and no longer train like they did in their youth, if they kept up with the same eating strategies they had, that muscle turns to fat. There are a lot of great vegan athletes out there, some of whom have retired and they seem to maintain their physique pretty well or at least appear lean and fit.

You could eat nothing but fruit, which is low in protein, and take in enough calories and protein for a day according to the RDA. Also check out https://cronometer.com if you want to have a great resource that will tell you what your macro and micronutrient intake for the day is. I definitely recommend trying out this site. It breaks down your food intake in a day and shows you if you are eating a balanced diet. It has a few minor flaws, but for the most part I think it is a great site! With that said, there are a number of whole, plant-based foods that are high in protein.

Beans: black, red, soy, chickpea, pinto, kidney, etc.

Legumes: peanuts, peas, carob

Nuts: pecans, almonds, pine nuts, walnuts, Brazil nuts, etc.

Seeds: quinoa (actually a seed), sunflower, sesame, flax, hemp, etc.

Grains: brown rice, millet, wheat, buckwheat, corn, oats, barley, etc.

Dark leafy greens: collard, kale, spinach, arugula, etc.

This is a short list but it gives you an idea. There are plenty of lightly processed vegan foods that are also packed with protein which include: whole wheat or quinoa pasta, tofu (soy product), seitan (wheat gluten), and some vegan faux meat products.

The second macronutrient that is found in all foods is fat. Fat is a necessary component of our diet and certainly one that is consumed in more than ideal amounts in modern societies. Fat plays a role in absorbing certain nutrients or fat-soluble vitamins such as A, D, E and K. It also helps insulate our bodies and keeps us warm. In addition to that, fat is secondary source of energy in the absence of carbohydrates. The problem is exceeding the amount of fat that the body needs. Because of the rich, western diet with a focus on animal foods, processed foods and the lack of fibrous foods, we have had an epidemic of diet related disease. High fat diets are associated with heart disease, Type 2 Diabetes and certain forms of cancer. We can avoid a lot of these issues by eating a diet higher in complex carbohydrate foods such as roots, grains, beans and tubers, rounded out with leafy greens, starchy vegetables and fruits.

Again, be aware of vegetable oil in processed foods and in your own cooking. It is pure fat and can even cause harm to people that follow a standard vegan diet that simply avoids animal foods. Added fat in this form can raise cholesterol levels and lead to heart disease even with groups that don't ingest any dietary cholesterol.

But what about olive oil, is that ok? There was short-term research done on olive oil that suggested that it lowered the bad cholesterol and raised the good. A lot of people including many doctors took this information and ran with it, advising people that it is a healthy fat because the study got a lot of press. People like to hear good things about their bad habits. There were more long-term studies done with controlled groups having either saturated fat (animal fat, coconut oil, etc.) added to their diet, which had already proven to raise total cholesterol levels, and a group consuming mono-unsaturated oil (olive oil). In the same study, both groups had equally bad cholesterol at the end and during angiograms; the coronary disease progressed just as much in each group[12].

So how do we consume fat and get what our body needs without harming ourselves? Try to avoid animal fats, vegetable oils, and limit your amount of nuts, seeds and avocados. Too many nuts and seeds can also be a problem especially if you are prone to heart disease. It is easy to over eat these, especially in the form of nut butters or when canned and with their tough shells removed. If we actually tried to eat a cup of nuts with their shells on them, it would be a lot more labor intensive and we probably wouldn't eat as many. But when all the work is removed, it is easy to binge eat on these by the handful.

Fat is good but we get plenty of our recommended fat by sticking with an array of fruits, vegetables, whole grains, beans, roots, tubers and sparse helpings of nuts and seeds. If you are used to making a stir-fry or a soup that starts off with sautéed vegetables in a pot with some

---

[12] Killoran,Eugenia. *Pritikin Weight Loss Resort*, 4 Sept. 2016, www.pritikin.com/your-health/healthy-living/eating-right/1103-whats-wrong-with-olive-oil.html. Accessed 08/07/2017

vegetable oil, try sautéing with just a bit of water or vegetable stock on a non-stick surface. I do this all of the time now and I don't miss the added fat.

There are many ways to incorporate healthy fat in a whole-foods, plant-based form. I usually start my day off with some oatmeal mixed with banana, berries, cinnamon and a few ground up pumpkin seeds, walnuts, ground flax seed or peanuts. It's delicious and a great way to incorporate a small amount of concentrated plant fat into your diet. It is also easy to eat this way on tour as I mentioned before. This is probably the ultimate tour meal because of the ease of preparation and because it stays within the whole-foods, plant-based philosophy of eating.

Below is a list of foods that contain healthy fats in their whole-food forms. Remember to eat these sparingly, and that it isn't necessary to eat these daily to consume enough dietary fat. Also note that even unlikely fruits, grains and vegetables all have nominal amounts of fat that will contribute to your total intake, so it isn't necessary to consume a lot of additional fats in order maintain healthy dietary fat levels. Again, check out cronometer.com and you'll be able to see how easy it is to meet your recommended daily levels of fat and also how easy it is to overdo it on the Standard American Diet.

Nuts: walnuts, almonds, pecans, pine nuts, Brazil Nuts, Hazelnuts, etc.

Seeds: sunflower, flax, hemp, pumpkin, sesame, etc.

Fruits: avocado, durian, olive, etc.

Legumes/Beans: peanut, soy bean.

The third macronutrient to discuss is carbohydrate. Simply put, carbohydrates are the biological molecule containing carbon, hydrogen and oxygen atoms. Carbohydrates break down into simple sugars within the body and are used to fuel every cell in the body. Whole food carbohydrates should be the center of our diet. We need these foods for energy to do physical activity as well as for involuntary activity.

Being a drummer, which is a very physical and mentally taxing activity, I need a lot of energy in the form of carbohydrates to perform and practice every day. Even before I was a drummer, I was a swimmer as a child and I remember at an early age having these big meals of spaghetti the night before a race. Even though I wouldn't recommend this now, we'd eat simple carbohydrate foods such as candy, "pixie sticks," moments before a race. Consuming pure carbohydrate or sugar into your system, without any fiber or phytochemicals that join in, causes the sugar to rapidly absorb in your system. You also get a dose of unwanted food additives such as artificial colors, flavors and preservatives. Needless to say, having a quick shot of glucose in my system, right before a competition, wouldn't weigh me down and would give me a quick jolt of energy. The power of drugs is strong. Of course there is a crash afterwards when you consume pure carbohydrate like this. It is better to have a ripe banana or maybe a mango or some other sweet fruit with all of its fiber intact before a race, or in my case, before a show.

Not much has really changed over the years with this concept. Sure, in recent times there have been dietary trends that damn carbohydrates, but many endurance athletes (or in my case drummers who are basically athletes), welcome healthy doses of carbohydrates to help fuel their performance.

When it comes to healthy carbohydrate sources, I highly recommend choosing whole food sources, for example:

Fruit: bananas, peaches, apples, plums, melons, oranges, grapefruit, mangos, berries, grapes, jackfruit, dates, etc. The list is way too long!!

Grains: brown rice, millet, whole wheat, buckwheat, rye, oats, barley, corn, teff, etc.

Roots, tubers and starchy vegetables: Potatoes, sweet potatoes, butternut squash, yams, yucca, pumpkin, beets, carrots, etc.

This should be the bulk of the human diet. I believe that we evolved to eat this way and so long as this is the center point of your diet, you'll enjoy maximum health benefits and have energy to do whatever you want and need to do during the day.

Micronutrients

If you consume a whole-food, plant-based diet with the focus on high-carbohydrate whole foods with some added leaves, seeds and nuts, you'll take in all your body needs as far as micronutrients, antioxidants and phytochemicals are concerned. Micronutrients are chemical compounds that the human body requires in trace amounts in order to function in a healthy manner. Vitamins and minerals make up these chemical compounds. I will focus on the two micronutrients that can sometimes be a problem with any diet, not just a plant-based one. The two vitamins are B12 and D. As I mentioned earlier, vitamin D can be an issue to those living in the northern parts of the globe, where during the winter months, sunlight exposure is minimal. Our body creates it when our skin is exposed to a moderate amount of sunlight. A lot of sources say that 10 minutes of sun exposure on your hands and face every day should be sufficient[13]. As I mentioned earlier, if you don't have access to some adequate sunlight, there are supplements you can take and some foods are fortified with it, like various non-dairy milks and cereals.

Vitamin B12 is created by bacteria that live in our soil and streams.[14] It is stored within the tissues of the

---

[13] "How Do I Get the Vitamin D My Body Needs?" *Vitamin D Council*, www.vitamindcouncil.org/about-vitamin-d/how-do-i-get-the-vitamin-d-my-body-needs/. Accessed 08/07/2017

[14] Office, Anne Trafton News. "MIT Biologists Solve Vitamin Puzzle." *MIT News*, 21 Mar. 2007, news.mit.edu/2007/b12. Accessed 08/07/2017

farm animals that graze upon the unwashed vegetation in the soil and that drink from streams. Modern factory farmed animals are typically supplemented with Vitamin B12 in their feed or via injections because they are eating a more sterile diet and aren't able to graze in the fields. Vitamin B12 deficiency can also become a problem for vegans long-term because of modern farming practices and from modern ways of living. Humans used to be in closer contact with our food, but through years of depleting our soil and sanitizing our produce, Vitamin B12 has become a difficult nutrient to take in. We also used to drink from the streams which contained Vitamin B12 as well, but our streams have become so polluted that I would not advise this, nor is it practical in modern times when most of us live in a city. The flipside to our lack of natural Vitamin B12 in our water supply is that we don't experience cholera like we may have during our pre-sanitization of water days, so it is better to just take a supplement in this case.

There are a few sources of Vitamin B12 in the plant world may need a bit more research that are speculated to contain the nutrient, but as of now it is considered an unreliable source. These sources include sea vegetables, brewer's yeast, fermented foods such as sauerkraut or kimchi, tempeh (fermented soy cake), chlorella, and spirulina (blue green algae). It is good to add these foods to your diets, but I'd still say it is a good idea to supplement your diet with a sublingual (rests under your tongue until dissolved) pill form of Vitamin B12.

Vitamin B12 deficiency can become a problem for people that are on a long term vegan diet and can lead to weakness, tiredness, yellowed skin (jaundice), anemia, numbness or tingling in the hands, legs or feet, paranoia, or difficulty thinking. The body stores Vitamin B12 in the liver and a deficiency may not appear for 20 to 30 years.[15]Vegan or not, when visiting a doctor for lab tests, it is a good idea to check your Vitamin B12 levels. I have done this and fortunately have maintained positive levels over the years as a long-term vegan.

If you have a Vitamin B12 deficiency you can reverse it with weekly shots of Vitamin B12 or heavy doses of sublingual B12 pills. They are fairly affordable and are water-soluble, so whatever the body doesn't use or store gets excreted through your urine. There has been no sign of danger of overdosing on this vitamin so many experts believe it to be safe to consume.

As a precaution to Vitamin B12 deficiency, I take a sublingual pill in the form of methylcobalamin or cyanocobalamin twice a week. These are very high doses and our bodies do a good job of storing a surplus of this nutrient in our liver. I have noticed there is a debate over which form of B12 is best to take. Dr. Michael Greger thinks the research out their favors cyanocobalamin where Dr. Alan Goldhamer has favored methylcobalamin. I respect both of these doctors and until I have better information, I alternate between the two forms. Again, this is an inexpensive vitamin supplement, so having a bottle of each on hand won't cost much more than $15 and should last you a year or longer.

Another micronutrient of concern in this diet is sodium in the form of added dietary salt. Sodium breaks

---

[15] Digestion, Absorption, and Transport." *Digestion, Absorption, and Transport of B12*, veganhealth.org/b12/dig. Accessed 08/07/2017

down the cell walls of the food we eat quickly, bringing out the flavor of the food in a more concentrated form, which appeals to our senses. There is debate on whether it is more beneficial to incorporate it into our diets or to just consume it naturally with our food. Most green vegetables such as kale, celery, and spinach as well as sea vegetables will contain adequate amounts of sodium for our diet without the harmful chloride element that is contained in table salt.[16] I find that if you are preparing your own food, you should try to do as many low salt or salt-free dishes as possible. Your taste buds will adjust over time. It may seem bland at first, but in a matter of weeks, you won't miss it. I have been lowering my salt intake over the years and I now barely use any when cooking. In many cases don't add any at all.

When traveling, I'm more likely to encounter more sodium in the form of table salt in my diet because of catered meals and restaurants, but I counter this as much as possible by my eating habits while at home. The problem with too much salt is that if you're at risk, it can lead to hypertension, abnormal heart development and contribute to osteoporosis. On the flipside, experts in nutrition and medicine like Dr. John McDougall believe that his patients can add a little salt to their meals in order for them to maintain a starch-focused diet that is void of animal foods and oils. Adding a little salt to the surface of your food simply makes it more palatable, but again, your taste buds adjust as you begin to lower your salt content. If you can do a "no table salt" diet, go for it. You will not be deficient in sodium if green vegetables and seaweed

[16] TheCoolVegetarian. "Are Oils & Salts Healthy ? - Dr. Alan Goldhamer."*YouTube*, YouTube, 12 Sept. 2011, www.youtube.com/watch?v=2L7wN2ORHXU.

are consumed regularly, but it is certainly more important for your health to eliminate animal foods and vegetable oils. If the food tastes too bland at first, add a pinch of salt to it or a simple condiment like hot sauce to help add a bit of flavor to your meal. It will certainly help with transitioning over to eating this way and sustaining this lifestyle long-term.

Heart disease runs in my father's side of the family, so I try to minimize the amount of sodium in my diet, but I occasionally use a little sea salt here and there when cooking. It has drastically decreased over the years though and I find myself often eating meals without salt now and enjoying them just the same. I really only add salt if I am making a big soup dish and the whole pot as a simple dash of salt added when I am starting it off.

As far as the other common vitamins and minerals go, they come in abundance in all plant life and if you are eating whole foods, you should be getting plenty of everything else that you need and won't ever have to worry about deficiencies. Again, I highly urge people to check out www.chronometer.com if you are interested in seeing the nutritional breakdown of what you are consuming in a day. You'll find it difficult to be deficient in anything as long as you focus on whole, plant foods.

Although the research is still developing, it is believed that plants contain powerful health benefits in the form of phytochemicals. Phytochemicals are chemical compounds that occur naturally in plants. We have heard of carotenoids in carrots, which make them orange, having anti-cancer properties and flavonoids in blueberries that also help with suppressing cancer and inflammation.

There is still a lot of research to be done in this field but many believe that these are powerful, health promoting properties within plants and that each plant contains unique phytochemicals based on their color, scent and taste.

Antioxidants are molecules that inhibit the oxidation of other molecules. Oxidation creates free radicals that damage cells that can lead to cancer within the body. Plant foods contain an array of antioxidants such as vitamin A, C and E. All plant foods contain these powerful nutrients. Eat a wide variety of plant foods and your body will benefit from the antioxidants within them.

I'm sure with time we'll be hearing more about the science behind antioxidants and phytochemicals but there is still much research to be done. There has been a lot of correlation between high plant consumption and lower cancer rates. Vegan or not, experts will agree to consume a high amount of fruits and vegetables in various colors to benefit from their phytochemicals.

Chapter 5
Veganism for the Animals

Chances are if you are reading this you've already educated yourself and formulated opinions about animal rights. I think it is natural for most humans to feel a certain level of compassion towards animals, whether the individual decides to go vegan or not. Most of us abhor mistreatment of our own species and other species when encountered with it face to face. It makes us uncomfortable. So we tend to take an "out of sight, out of mind" approach when dealing with the suffering in the world, be it animals or fellow humans in order to not feel depressed all day long.

I've never really been in a fight before, but one time I was walking down the main street area on Ohio State's campus when a fight spilled out of a bar. There was a young man getting badly beaten into the concrete and without fail, I stepped in to pull the aggressor off of him, which in turn started a chain reaction of other bystanders stepping in and separating the two. We all felt it. Who knows why this person was getting his ass kicked so badly? It didn't matter though. We all felt the need to protect this guy that simply couldn't defend himself any longer. I think most people would do something similar if faced with this directly because we all have at least some level of compassion and empathy.

The same goes for animals. Most of us love cats and dogs and we have them as pets. I explained my guinea pig story earlier, but I can recall seeing violence against a dog outside of a punk rock show as a teenager. Some other people and I stepped in to intervene when a guy was beating his dog aggressively to reprimand him for whatever he did. At one point, the guy picked his dog up by the collar he had on and the dog yelped loudly. The guy ended up wanting to fight us for calling him out, and that took a bit of yelling back and forth, but the take-home is that we all felt uncomfortable with his actions towards this animal. We stepped in to stop the abuse that was happening directly in front of us. These examples are demonstrations of compassion that most people possess. Nobody likes to see someone dominate over another whether it's a human or an animal. We all feel compassionate for the person or animal that is at the mercy of the dominating force.

Humans have been eating animals for centuries and I don't think I or anyone else could ever convince everyone on the planet not to do it anymore. A lot of people that partake in consuming animals think it is necessary for survival and that we are designed to do so. Not to mention, most of us were born and raised to eat animals and making a major change towards a plant-based lifestyle can be a huge undertaking. It will take more scientific evidence to convince people to either cut back or eliminate their meat consumption. I don't believe that a gory slaughterhouse video will work on everyone because of the varying degrees of compassion people possess.

So what is wrong with modern animal agriculture? Regardless of whether or not you think it is ok for an animal to be held captive by humans and eventually slaughtered for its meat, modern animal agriculture is far from what a lot of people believe it to be. Back in the day, cows, chickens and pigs would roam free on a plot of land, able to feed off of grass and seeds that have fallen from trees. When you drive along the freeway, you'll occasionally see this set-up where there are just a handful of cows in a nice green pasture, grazing in the sun. Even though those cows are what end up providing milk or steak later on, they seem to live a good chunk of their life in peace, but most animal agriculture is not like this at all.

In modern times, we treat our animals like commodities throughout their whole existence. Animals that are raised for food purposes live in unsightly conditions on factory farms. They are fed a diet that forces them to grow and fatten up quickly, so that they can then be slaughtered for our consumption. It is all about maximum production with minimal cost. If you don't believe me, check out any of the documentaries out there on slaughterhouses. I recommend "Earthlings." At a young age, those "Faces Of Death" documentaries contained slaughterhouse footage as well and if that doesn't disturb you on some level, then maybe my idea that we as humans have levels of compassion is wrong.

Don't we need to eat meat for protein, iron and nutrients we can't get from plants? The answer is no. Name one person with a protein deficiency living in an industrialized society. It is probably difficult. Plants give you all the essential nutrients that we could possibly need: all of the amino acids that are the building blocks of protein, iron, B-vitamins and anything else, minus the dietary cholesterol and high amounts of saturated fat. This is especially true with an oil-free, plant-based, whole-foods diet.

If you aren't considering ever giving up meat full time, consider at least cutting down. Animal agriculture, like any large industry, operates according to supply and demand. The more we demand meat, the more we're going to have to figure out short-cuts to raising animals with minimal costs. Also, consider organic or meat from the local farmer's market. In a lot of these cases, the conditions that these animals live in are at least a little better before their ultimate demise. They are also less likely to have harmful antibiotics and hormones, added to keep them growing fast and with less sickness, that we end up consuming in the muscle tissue of the animal in concentrated amounts.

As I write this, science continues to develop and there is a team of scientists attempting to create meat in a lab that is real meat without the suffering of animals. They are developing this technology using stem cells from the animals and growing it in a lab. The push behind this technology is to meet our ever-growing meat demands and provide an alternative that is cheaper, with less of a negative environmental impact and involves no suffering of the animals. I think this is a great concept and we'll see where it goes. I still would not consume this product because I am still of the belief that we aren't really designed to consume animal products, but for those out there that simply won't give up meat, I think this is an amazing alternative. I'd love to fast forward and see the outcome of this science experiment. I'm most excited that I would no longer have to support the meat/dairy industry when it comes to feeding the cats that I foster and have adopted. If they could have an alternative that fits with their carnivore diet where I don't have to support factory farming, I will definitely take this route, provided that it won't cause any suffering to the cats in any way. Time will only tell.

I won't spend too much time here because I think you have to really look inside yourself to see if you can live with partaking in the enslavement and suffering of another animal. If you can, carry on, but maybe also consider the health issues and environmental issues that also come with the animal food industry. Also, spend some time near a farm, if you can. Hang out with a cow or a pig. They are benevolent creatures that feel similar feelings that we do. I went to go see Joan Jett perform at the Orange County fair a couple of years ago and with my ticket, I got to hang out at the fair as well. Part of the fair was a small petting zoo and the agricultural sector that had cows, chickens and pigs on display. I watched all of the families get so excited to interact and pet these animals. Without a doubt, most of the adults were thinking "this will be my burger later," and I heard so many conversations of parents discussing that with their children. What a great case for veganism? The children weren't too thrilled about this concept after getting to see these majestic animals face to face. We'll see how things go for the next generation. Maybe there will be less animal consumption, less destruction of land due to animal agriculture, and more plants and fruit-bearing trees instead. That would be wonderful!

Chapter 6
Veganism for the Environment

More and more, the world is getting hit with the problem that we're heading towards in regards to polluting the environment. We're using up the Earth's resources at an alarming rate, and the growing amount of greenhouse gases are destroying our ozone layer and contributing to global warming. Part of this is due to overpopulation and the demands that it has with the Earth's resources. Most people believe it was because of the automobile industry but it has been documented that the large portion of this destructive gas that is destroying the ozone is due to factory farming and the methane that is produced by all of the farm animals that we raise for food. The 2006 report from the United Nations brought this information to the masses about the destruction of our environment due to animal agriculture and urged people to cut back on meat consumption. Now you see a lot of people taking a moderate approach towards veganism with "Meatless Mondays" and other such attempts to cut back on our mass consumption of meat. Check out the fantastic documentary "Cowspiracy" on the subject if you'd like to dive further into the environmental impact of the animal agriculture industry on our planet.

For some time now, people in wealthier societies have been able to gorge themselves with meat and animal products while the poorer countries rely on grain based diets to survive. Meat has always been a status symbol in a lot of cultures. If you could afford meat, especially the more sought after components of the cow, it was a sign of wealth and prosperity on some level. On the other hand in poorer societies, or even the poor in wealthier societies (like the Roman gladiators who were slaves that were used for entertainment battles), were fed a diet based around rich starchy vegetables. Their main staple was barley and they were considered the strongest people around at the time. They were also called "The Barley Men." They had very little animal protein in their diet, if any at all, but were healthy and exuded tremendous strength and could withstand hours of rigorous training each day on this starch-centered diet.

These days it is common in wealthy societies to have meat and animal products be the center of each meal of the day. For breakfast, its bacon and eggs, with toast and butter, and coffee with cream. For lunch, it is a burger, fries and a shake and for dinner it is a steak, chicken or a piece of fish with baked potato, butter and sour cream and a side of asparagus. Even for snacks, we'll have ice cream, cookies, and candy. In less developed countries, people generally follow their traditional diets, although that is slowly changing as globalization occurs and fast food companies start to influence the eating strategies. In those countries, the traditional diets tend to focus on a grain or a starch as the centerpiece. In some cases meat or animal products are used in small amounts but it is more of a condiment in size compared to what the rich western diet is accustomed to.

Now, in order to keep up with the demand of animal food products globally, we have done a lot of nasty things to our environment in order to meet these demands. We've been using up tons of farmland in

America for corn and other animal feed to grow, where we could be using that corn or land to plant other vegetables for humans. We've been clear cutting rainforests in South America to make room for animal agriculture production because most of the grain that is produced in the US goes to feeding livestock. We go to other countries and buy out their land to produce cattle, etc., just to satisfy demand for meat in the US.

Eating meat and animal products is contributing largely to the destruction of our planet. If feeling compassionate towards animals by not eating them has no interest to you, at least consider the effects of spending your money on a burger versus some hearty vegetarian chili, or if you're transitioning over, a veggie burger. By the time we have grandchildren, they may not get to see the beautiful rainforests of South America or the glaciers in the Arctic regions due to global warming. We may only get to see those ecosystems remembered in "Planet Earth" style programming. Also, who knows what it will do to the global ecosystems when all that unique plant and animal life goes extinct because of clear-cutting? We'll certainly have less bio-diversity.

The statistics go on. Livestock production is responsible for 64% of the ammonia that enters our environment, causing acid rain. Livestock production also is responsible for 65% of the greenhouse gas nitrous oxide from all of the manure from these animals. When you look at the amount of fresh water it takes to produce a kilogram of beef verses a pound of wheat, the results are eye opening as well. For one kilogram of beef it takes anywhere from 13,000 to 100,000 liters of water and for one kilogram of wheat it takes 1000-2000 liters.[17] The carbon footprint of someone following a simple, healthy, vegetarian diet is drastically lower than that of an omnivore.

It doesn't end here though. We have to use a lot more pesticides that run off and pollute our rivers, oceans and streams when we're spraying all of those cornfields that produce our livestock feed. If we simply ate the corn ourselves, we wouldn't have so much extra pesticide run-off in our streams, rivers and oceans that contaminate our water and destroy those ecosystems and also the fish that we all eat. When you eat fish, cows, chickens or pigs, you're eating all of that pesticide build-up as well. In addition to pesticide run-off you have all of the manure from these animals that runs off into our streams and waterways as well. It destroys our topsoil and pollutes the air as well as our waterways. Methane gas from cattle production is a major contributor to global warming and is considered a greenhouse gas.

Not only are we destroying our environment, but all of the hormones and antibiotics that we inject into our livestock get concentrated into the tissue of the animals that we consume, and we get them in heavy doses, which are believed to cause certain forms of cancer as well as reproductive dysfunction. As for our oceans are concerned, we are experiencing a drastic decrease in aquatic life due to over-fishing, and we're not allowing enough time to rebuild our sea life populations before we

---

[17] Tinawi, Antoine. "Acid Rain Livestock Generates 64%." *LinkedIn SlideShare*, 6 June 2009, www.slideshare.net/vegetarian108/101-reasons-to-go-vegetaian/26-Acid_Rain_Livestock_generates_64. Accessed 08/09/2017

go back in with nets, scooping up what is left. It's a sad state for our oceans and seas.

Consider a vegan diet for the sake of the earth that we all live in. A diet that centers itself on whole foods that are of plant origin is not only good for the animals, but also better for us and better for the environment we live in, especially as our global population increases. As the population increases, so will the demands for food. We can't eat this rich western diet for decades to come without major environmental repercussions, so even if going vegan will never be your thing, at least consider looking more towards plants being the bulk of your diet. It will help your health and the world. Even Arnold Schwarzenegger of all people has spoken out in favor of consuming more plants and less meat for the environment. This is really becoming a mainstream issue, not just one that is talked about amongst vegans and environmentalists.

Chapter 7
Veganism May be the Most Fitting Diet for Humans

After much reading and life experience, I truly believe that eating a whole-food, plant-based diet is the ideal way of eating for humans at all stages of life. If you compare our anatomy to that of herbivore animals, omnivore animals and carnivore animals we share most common traits with the herbivore.

	Carnivores	Omnivores	Herbivores	Humans
Facial muscles	Reduced to allow wide mouth gape	Reduced	Well-developed	Well-developed
Jaw type	Angle not expanded	Angle not expanded	Expanded angle	Expanded angle
Jaw joint location	On same plane as molar teeth	On same plane as molar teeth	Above the plane of the molars	Above the plane of the molars
Jaw motion	Shearing; minimal side-to-side motion	Shearing; minimal side-to-side motion	No shear; good side-to-side, front to back	No shear; good side-to-side, front to back
Major jaw muscles	Temporalis	Temporalis	Masseter and pterygoids	Masseter and pterygoids
Mouth opening vs. head size	Large	Large	Small	Small
Teeth: Incisors	Short and pointed	Short and pointed	Broad, flattened and spade shaped	Broad, flattened and spade shaped
Teeth: Canines	Long, sharp and curved	Long, sharp and curved	Dull and short or long (for defense), or none	Short and blunted
Teeth: Molars	Sharp, jagged and blade shaped	Sharp blades and/or flattened	Flattened with cusps vs. complex	Flattened with nodular cusps

				surface
Chewing	None; swallows food whole	Swallows food whole and/or simple crushing	Extensive chewing necessary	Extensive chewing necessary
Saliva	No digestive enzymes	No digestive enzymes	Carbohydrate digesting enzymes	Carbohydrate digesting enzymes
Stomach type	Simple	Simple	Simple or multiple chambers	Simple
Stomach Capacity	60% to 70% of total volume of digestive tract	60% to 70% of total volume of digestive tract	Less than 30% of total volume of digestive tract	21% to 27% of total volume of digestive tract
Stomach acidity, with food in stomach	Less than or equal to pH 1 with food in stomach	Less than or equal to pH 1 with food in stomach	pH 4 to 5 with food in stomach	pH 4 to 5 with food in stomach
Length of small intestine	3 to 6 times body length	4 to 6 times body length	10 to more than 12 times body length	10 to 11 times body length
Colon	Simple, short and smooth	Simple, short and smooth	Long, complex; may be sacculated	Long, sacculated
Liver	Can detoxify vitamin A	Can detoxify vitamin A	Cannot detoxify vitamin A	Cannot detoxify vitamin A
Kidney	Extremely concentrated urine	Extremely concentrated urine	Moderately concentrated urine	Moderately concentrated urine
Nails	Sharp claws	Sharp claws	Flattened nails or blunt hooves	Flattened nails[18]

If we were really designed to eat animal protein, then why are we faced with so many diet-related health issues? In a speech from animal rights activist Gary Yourofsky on veganism, he brought up a challenge to test if we are carnivores, omnivores or herbivores by design. He mentioned that we should go outside right now, hunt down a squirrel, capture it with our mouths, rip open its

---

[18] Mills, Milton R. *The Comparative Anatomy of Eating*, www.ecologos.org/anatomy.htm. Accessed 08/14/2017

flesh and consume all of the parts raw; the blood, the brains, the intestines, the anus, and do this day after day.[19] I don't think we'd have too many volunteers. Also, put a two-year old child in a room with an apple and a bunny rabbit. Will the child eat the apple and play with the bunny rabbit or vice versa? If it does the later, then I will reconsider my stance.

I'll put my own two cents in on this and say that we had a fly zipping around our apartment the other day and my cat, Luna, was chasing it for minutes. She finally caught the fly and ate it right up, whole. I can't think of many people that would relish the idea of capturing a fly like this and consuming it.

I believe that eventually there will be a shift towards a plant-based diet due to the ever-growing evidence of the harmful effects of meat, dairy and eggs not just on people, but also on the environment. It almost seems like a no brainer for anyone who is following the science and has compassion for animals. For a long time, cigarette smoking was not considered harmful even though we had scientific evidence to the contrary. The statistics were high that the average person smoked 4000 cigarettes per year (half a pack a day). Our physicians and media were telling people to smoke decades ago because there wasn't any data going against it in the mainstream media. There were plenty of advertisements out there making people believe they'd be super cool if they smoked cigarettes even though we had scientific evidence in the 30's that let us know that cigarette smoking was

---

[19] TheAnimalHolocaust, and Gary Yourofsky. "Best Speech You Will Ever Hear - Gary Yourofsky." *YouTube*, YouTube, 23 Dec. 2010, www.youtube.com/watch?v=es6U00LMmC4. Accessed 08/16/2017

associated with lung cancer. Now you have these massive bold print messages on cigarette boxes warning us about the harmful effects of smoking. I wonder if the same will happen with meat.

Recently, processed meat (chicken nuggets, hot dogs, bologna, etc.) has been labeled, "a first-class carcinogen" by the surgeon general, yet we still feed these foods to our children in schools. I wonder if that will ever come with a gargantuan warning on the packaging, similar to cigarette packaging, and we'll switch to healthier food choices. It seems to be getting worse with fast food chains infiltrating schools with their garbage food. This food is a drug. It has the same effects as heroin[20], yet most people blindly consume it regularly and we see the consequences of it regularly with the American people in the form of obesity and diet-related illness. It is absolutely horrendous that we set up the youth with such horrible habits at an early age.

It all comes down to money. These companies have so much money that they are able to pay for influence in the political fields and in our educational fields. The best way to combat it is with your dollar. Don't support these horrible industries if at all possible and if you do, buy their plant-based products. These people are in it for money and if they see a switch going on, they'll follow. I don't believe people wake up every morning like

---

[20] Hough, Andrew. "Junk Food 'as Addictive as Heroin and Smoking'." *The Telegraph*, Telegraph Media Group, 29 Mar. 2010, www.telegraph.co.uk/news/health/news/7533668/Junk-food-as-addictive-as-heroin-and-smoking.html.

an evil villain, thinking "How can I harm a million people today?" I believe that they are thinking, "How can I make a ton of money?"

Back when my father was alive he had open-heart surgery in his early 40's. I had no idea what this meant at the time and I didn't know of anyone else's father needing such an invasive form of surgery. I think a lot of my current views on nutrition and veganism stem from not wanting to follow in his footsteps. He golfed a little and would mow the lawn occasionally, (we had a riding mower, by the way,) and that is about it as far as exercise for his heart went. He also would eat burgers, fries, shakes, soft drinks, frozen pizzas and little in the way of plant food, which contributed to his obesity and heart issues. As I have started to approach his age, I really feel better about the diet strategy that I have because I don't want the high cholesterol that he had. In fact, I remember after his open-heart surgery, my family pushed to get my cholesterol levels checked as a kid and it was over 200, which is horrible for a 12-year-old. I wasn't obese but I was already developing heart issues at a young age following a similar diet, with the addition of candy and unhealthy snacks. Luckily with my no oil, low salt, whole-foods, plant-based diet, along with exercise, I have kept my cholesterol levels and triglyceride levels in the low range.

For most people, it will take a life threatening event like open-heart surgery to bring about lifestyle changes, but we live in a world where drugs are advertised everywhere we go on TV, the internet, magazines and even in the doctor's office in the form of pamphlets in the waiting room and posters on the wall. We're such a pill and potion society that we'd rather just do that than make a few lifestyle adjustments that could alter our course in life. It is like having a sink overflowing water onto the floor and all we do is mop it up as opposed to fixing the sink. We need to fix our diets and lifestyle, not treat our bad habits with pills and procedures. That should only be a last ditch effort after making changes to the way we live first. Doctors and pharmaceutical companies are out to make money through procedures and pills, not by telling people to not eat oil and to eat more nutrient rich kale. We've all heard of big-pharma but certainly not big-kale. There is more money for pharmaceutical companies to make by keeping people sick. Doctors get paid for medical procedures, not for advising people to eat diets that are plant-based and can reverse most modern illnesses. There are good doctors out there though, and I do believe that the medical industry is necessary, especially when it comes to fixing acute problems, like a gunshot wound. But if we ate better, exercised, and had restful sleep, we would combat most of the issues that we see regularly in the doctor's office.

Also, I'd like to add that doctors aren't required to take lengthy courses on nutrition, so you can't always assume your doctor may understand nutrition better than your insurance salesman or your favorite drummer. ☺ Take control of your life and do a little research. If you see yourself going down a path where you are getting diagnosed with diet-related illness, make a change. Eating broccoli and sweet potatoes everyday is a lot less expensive than being in surgery, having your chest ripped open and having stents put into your heart.

Chapter 8
Taking Care of Myself Before a Tour

Before I get into what I eat on tour and how I take care of myself on the road, I want to explain how I live when I am not traveling. There are a few simple things I strive to do each day in order to maintain amazing health. Sometimes I fall short, but I try to do this each day, which I think is the most important thing. I absolutely love music, writing songs and drumming, all of which are very physically and mentally taxing, so it is crucial to have a lifestyle that supports my daily interests and optimizes my ability to perform my rituals.

For starters, I try to get plenty of sleep. I'm lucky right now because I am in the middle of a long tour. My day job is centered on being prepared for each upcoming leg of the tour, and since I'm well prepared, I have a bit more freedom that I am not used to having with my days. I don't set an alarm, but I do try to go to bed around the same time and I naturally wake up around the same time. I have cats and foster kittens, so often they will wake me up as the sun comes up to be fed their first meal of the day. This interrupts my sleep a little, but I have gotten better at falling back to sleep for a couple of hours after. Seven to eight hours seems to be the recommended dosage of sleep per day to function well, and I agree with that. You may actually need a little more if you really tax your body physically. I find that sometimes even nine hours of sleep each day helps me the most. If you start getting under seven, you run the risk of prematurely aging yourself and not being nearly as productive as you could be if you had more sleep. You've heard of getting beauty rest. It is definitely a real thing. The body needs solid sleep to rebuild tissue, improve memory function, grow muscle and synthesize hormones. In the modern world, this is tough, but do your best. I recommend blackout curtains too if you can have those in your living set-up. Some of my best sleep moments actually happen on tour in a hotel room, if I am given my own room with blackout curtains and a late lobby-call. I will sleep solidly in these situations because my cats aren't around to wake me up at dawn. They love playing tag with each other and their toys as the sun comes up and I am usually positioned in the middle of their playfield.

It wasn't too long ago that I was balancing a day job working for a local vegan restaurant in addition to practicing music daily, working-out and performing. It was extremely stressful and it forced me to be well organized in order to accomplish so much. Sleep was something that I neglected, and I was overworked. It took a bit of mind numbing activity (watching videos or documentaries) for me to relax towards bedtime each day. I believed that I had more of a challenge when it came time to practice my drums. I had a harder time focusing and I was tired and felt weak when it came to my stamina. Now that I get better sleep, I feel like I am more productive during my waking hours. Sleep is something that I find just as important as the food. Again, shoot for seven to eight hours per day and maybe more if you are physically active and need it and try to stay on somewhat of a schedule for best results. This clearly doesn't always work when on tour though. We'll get into that soon. When I get the opportunity, I don't take sleep for granted, especially as I get older.

Exercise is also a huge component of my life. It is kind of funny what inspired this but looking back, it was definitely a benefit. In college, I was in a long-term relationship with a girl for six and a half years and we lived together. I ended up moving into her place somewhere in the middle of that and when we broke up, I had to move out. This came at a time in my life where I was in a major transition. I was touring quite a bit with my band, Mankind Is Obsolete, as well as drumming for a few other groups and teaching a few students, but I was dirt poor. I could barely pay rent and didn't have much money for food. I was surviving and being responsible, (paying my bills, etc.,) but I didn't have any room to breathe financially speaking. So when we broke up, I moved into my drum studio, which is a dark, hot, humid room within a big industrial warehouse. There were rats, cockroaches and lots of noise. I figured I could exist on a lot less money if I didn't have to rent an apartment in Los Angeles and also rent a drum studio as well, so even with the unsavory conditions, I lived in my drum studio because it made the most sense.

My strategy was to live in my drum studio, sleeping in there or in my van because of the noise, and take on some students and tours to finance it all. I acquired a gym pass so that I could shower every day. Back when I first had a drum studio in North Hollywood, there was this guy down the hall from me that lived out of his and he did the same while he worked on his music. I thought this was so cool that he had an affordable way of drumming and writing songs while living in a very expensive city. Looking back, I am amazed that I lasted 3 and a half years living like this, but I followed in his footsteps. Unfortunately, I had a guy try to break into the van I was sleeping in one night outside of the studio and that was a wake-up call to really work on revising my living situation. It took some time and a "day job" but I did eventually move out and rented my own place in addition to the studio. That's another story.

Let's get back to the living in the studio days because it is an important role and a foundation for how I live today. So here I am Jon "scrawny vegan" Siren showing up at the gym for the first time, mostly to shower but I did have a bit of an open mind to having better fitness. It was intimidating being amongst some very massive dudes who were power lifting. I dove in headfirst though and began a regimen of fifteen minutes of cardio machines, five minutes of stretching and thirty minutes of strength training. My reward was a shower, and I had to do this at least 6 days a week because I needed to show up to work looking and smelling clean. It wasn't long before I developed a genuine passion and enthusiasm towards physical fitness.

Exercise doesn't have to be going to the gym, though. I do believe that it is a part of a healthy lifestyle and the side effects are all positive. My drumming has improved because of the endurance and strength that I have developed in my arms and legs. It was also a great way to warm up and jumpstart my day. I think it added to my mental clarity as well. Focusing on drumming or writing became easier after a gym session.

I absolutely love going to the gym now. This is something that I would have probably never said before and I never envisioned myself doing so as a child. I used to hate it in high school, especially because I think I was the last guy in my class to hit puberty. My peers were able to outperform me in any sport related activity where at one time I had a good chance. I think my self-esteem wasn't too high either around that time because of this lack of becoming a "man" yet. I can recall not taking gym classes until late in my high school years because I didn't have faith in my abilities anymore. In order to graduate, the school told me that I had to work out with the football team in the mornings when they did their weight training because I hadn't taken enough gym classes. This was hilarious in hindsight. I can recall whoever had to be my partner for the day, rolling their eyes back because they'd have to take all of the weights off the barbell or other device each time in order for me to use the bench press machine or the leg press machine. It was tough. I laugh now, but at the time, being this scrawny vegan caused a good amount of ridicule in my environment. I took it pretty hard too, but I did learn a lot, and this knowledge has helped me to this day!

The good news is that I have moved past these difficult times of living out of my drum studio and showering at the gym. I took up a job doing all things "front-of-house" at a popular vegan restaurant in the Beverly Hills/West Hollywood area. They were very cool to me for a long time because they allowed me to work whenever I wasn't on a tour. I still wasn't making the kind of money one needs to survive on their own in Los Angeles playing music, but having this job really helped me during slow times. They also allowed me to take home a lot of food each night that was leftover from the day. A lot of it was very healthy food as well. I brought home all of the basics: quinoa, brown rice, beans, etc., and I would just need to supplement it with some fruits and vegetables. Also it was all organically grown, which was a bonus.

Even though I no longer live in my studio and shower at the gym, I still workout regularly. My fitness goals have evolved to fit my current lifestyle, but exercise has remained a part of my daily activity. I even stopped driving my car as much because I eventually no longer required my day job at the vegan restaurant. I get behind the wheel maybe twice per month in order to move drums or buy kitty litter in bulk and that is it. I travel around Los Angeles on my bicycle now. I love it! I get fresh air, a little sun, it takes me where I need to go and surprisingly fast too because I can scoot past most of the bad traffic. Most importantly, it adds to my exercise plan. I average about 10 miles on my bike every day. Now when I work out I just do a little five to ten minute jog on the treadmill before performing some strength exercises in my basement gym.

Even if the gym isn't your thing, humans need a bit of strength training and cardiovascular training. They are both important to bone, joint and heart health. You don't have to be a power lifter or a triathlon performer to get benefits either. Try going on a brisk walk or a jog for twenty to thirty minutes, three to five times per week and top it off with 30 push-ups, 30 squats, 30 lunges and 30 sit-ups. Do more if you'd like and go to one of those fitness parks where they have pull-up bars and dip bars. Add a few of those into the mix. My loft building has a couple of pieces of old gym equipment in the basement and I mostly just use that instead of paying additional cash for a gym membership. Also, in downtown Los Angeles there is a park that has some fitness gear in it where I can do chin-ups, pull-ups and dips. I ride past it when I go to my drum studio, so I stop by there for 5 or 10 minutes and add a quick workout on my way to or from the drum studio. If none of this sounds appealing at all, or maybe you are trying to add a little exercise into your life, I find that simply walking somewhere to take care of an errand is a great way to get exercise, sunlight and fresh air. It isn't going to make you sweat a ton or feel overworked. Try going to the grocery store and get a few things that you can fit in a backpack and then head home. I do that sometimes with my girlfriend because we can hangout, walk somewhere and get some fresh air, while running an errand. Just think of a way you can combine a few things and it won't really feel like exercise, but if you do it regularly, you will reap the rewards of moving your body consistently.

When I do all of this working out on a regular basis, my body is better equipped to handle the harsher conditions of touring. Give exercise a chance if it isn't part of your daily life already. Find something you love to do and change things up now and then so that it stays exciting. If you have to force yourself to do it after a couple of weeks, maybe it isn't the right thing for you. Some people need to work out alone: biking, swimming, running, weight training. Some prefer group classes like Pilates, aerobics, spin, yoga. Or maybe being part of a team activity is your thing, such as basketball, baseball, kickball, or soccer. All of these are good, but try something and do it a few times per week. Our bodies have not evolved to take escalators, sit on couches or at the computer all day long, order delivery meals and be as sedentary as we are today. All animals on this planet have to put a bit of muscle into their daily lives in order to survive and since we live in such an artificial environment of convenience, we're suffering the consequences. Start with a little physical exercise and try to incorporate more throughout the day. Take the stairs instead of the elevator. I take the stairs at least once per day and I live on the 12th floor of a building. By the time I hit the top. I get a little sweat on my brow. It feels good though and I love the way it keeps me trim. We all want nice bodies, and can have them with just a bit of work every day.

Mental health is something I focus on as well, especially when I am back in Los Angeles. Because of the suicide of my father and various aspects of my youth that brought about some unhealthy habits, I have been in therapy for many years. Therapy may be something that certain people turn their nose up at, but I'll have to say that I have had amazing results from taking care of all the baggage that I've had over the years. It has helped me in relationships and it is helping me with my self-esteem and with how I perceive life in general. If you are depressed and have been for a long time, or you had some trauma in your life, you know how debilitating that can be to fixate on these negative parts of your life on a daily basis. Get help and don't be ashamed of it. Finding a good therapist will help you work through the issues you have and give you an outlet for processing these dark thoughts. Even after years of therapy, I still go even though I feel well adjusted and I am no longer suicidal. I'm not a threat to myself any longer and I'm not a threat to others. I can perform my daily functions and I have an overall more positive outlook on life, but the therapy helps me maintain this. I'm sure that eventually there will come a day where I stop going.

It isn't easy to surrender yourself to help. I'll admit that, but when you do and you're open with a therapist, it can help you see the bigger picture of your life and help you function better. For a sizable chunk of my life, I'd have many moments where I just wanted to kill myself. I didn't have any faith in what I did or who I was. I blamed a lot of my poor outlook on life on my family upbringing and felt that I got a bad deck of cards to start off with. Over time, with some work, I have come to terms with a lot. I am more content with the person I am currently and what I went through to get here today and I think that anyone who is struggling with depression or suicidal thoughts should really consider professional help. I bring this up because it is all about the general health that I am trying to express here. Food, exercise, sleep and mental health are all important components to overall health and happiness. Maybe it is easy to compartmentalize these things like this, and that way one can take inventory on what they need to feel happy and healthy if they go through a few checkpoints. I think if you work on these things each day, you'll stand a better chance out in the world.

Lastly, what do I eat on a daily basis? My focus for a long time has been to eat the healthiest vegan diet that I can. It has been quite the evolution because digging through all of the clutter online and in books on healthy eating, plus my own experimenting has led me down a few different paths. I do believe that there is a correct diet for modern humans. I believe that evolution happens slowly and we have the anatomy that we have for a reason. I believe that we also have compassion for a reason too. This all confirms my vegan belief system, but not all vegan diets are the same. You can be the infamous "junk food vegan" who mimics modern unhealthy meat dishes using processed mock meats, tons of unhealthy fats in the form of oils or hydrogenated oil (margarine), excessive sodium (salt) and refined sugar. You can be vegan and eat a veggie burger, fries and chocolate soy shake, candy and processed, packaged snack cookies everyday and you'll encounter a lot of the same health problems that people following the Standard American Diet (SAD) do because of the refined sugar, excessive salt and vegetable oils. I used to do just this. I would eat a large cheese-free pizza and wash it down with that really cheap, disgusting green, purple or blue drink that comes in gallon milk containers for 99 cents in the dairy section of grocery stores. You've seen this abomination before if you live in the US and shop at conventional grocery stores. It contains no juice. It is simply a gallon of water with corn syrup, artificial flavors and dyes. It is horrible stuff but that was how I lived when I was 18 years old. My vegan, punk-rock buddies and I all ate this because it was so cheap, filling and released massive amounts of dopamine in our brains, getting us high. I had that deep fryer and would just deep fry batter dipped tofu with BBQ sauce and eat that with fries. It was vegan circus or carnival food! I'm happy I survived. Oh how ignorant was I back then?

I think maybe older age, not wanting to follow down the same pathway my father did, the feeling of my own mortality, or experiencing the food comas that I'd have after my body tried to process those horrible foods, has led me to a more healthy path. My current diet is a bit simpler and it centers around whole, plant foods with very little or no oil, little refined products, and trace amounts of salt or sugar added to certain things. I do have some vices as I've mentioned before. There is debate if coffee and alcohol should be included in a healthy diet.

You can find plenty of studies that lean in either direction, but one thing is for sure that both have consequences if done in excess and it is easy to do both in excess.

Every morning I enjoy a couple of cups of coffee to get started with my day. It doesn't seem to be a problem, and I'd like to see what more research has to say over the years. On the positive side of things, moderate coffee consumption may reduce the risk of developing Alzheimer's disease in the elderly. It also contains some powerful antioxidants that will help to ward off certain forms of cancer. It simply helps me to focus, first thing in the morning. So for now, I will continue drinking it, but I try to give myself a rest from it occasionally and I do notice a difference when I do. The flipside is coffee can be bad for people with high blood pressure or who have trouble sleeping, so it falls into the "handle with care" category for me. I enjoy it but may consider omitting it from my diet at some point. For now, my love for it still outweighs the seemingly mild consequences that are evident. If it becomes an issue, I'll lay this habit to rest for sure. For now, I think if people like coffee, treat it more like a treat and not something that should be consumed in large quantities.

The same goes for alcohol. I enjoy ending the night sometimes with a beer or two while on tour. If it has been a long and stressful day, a beer will relax me a bit and it feels good. I do know that I have to be adamant about cutting things off with two beers because anymore, I won't sleep well, I risk getting a hangover, and I risk saying stupid things in public. I know that can be fun and I think I am fun to be around when I am drunk, but my interest in having wild nights like that has slowly diminished over time. I'm more focused on music and my personal life, and boozing it up doesn't have as much of a spotlight anymore. I can easily see myself completely abstaining from alcohol in the future and lately it hasn't been an interest of mine to consume even in social situations.

So those are my vices. I try to limit them and when I do, it seems to have a positive effect on my body and mind. I'll now list out the healthy foods that I eat throughout the day, both in individual ways and in the form of a meal. Individually, I eat a lot of fruit, mainly bananas, berries of all sorts, pineapple, apples, oranges, grapefruit, tomatoes, cucumbers, mangos I'll also occasionally eat any other fruit out there, but these are the ones I eat the most of.

I eat a lot of beans and legumes, mostly pinto, black, kidney, mung, navy, chickpeas, peanuts, split peas (green and yellow) and lentils (brown and red). I eat a lot of grains and starches ("brown rice, corn, millet, quinoa, oats, barley, rye, wheat, buckwheat, potatoes, and sweet potatoes). I'll add to that pasta, but usually in whole grain form such as whole wheat, corn or quinoa. I do make or buy some breads or tortillas too. I like to buy sprouted grain bread and corn tortillas because they don't tend to add any oil. I also have a silicone bread loaf pan, with which I can make oil free quick breads, such as corn bread or even a lentil-based "meatloaf." I love these pans because they aren't harmful to the body with toxic residue and they are non-stick. Literally, nothing sticks to it. It is an amazing material and silicone cookware is cheap too!

I eat a ton of vegetables (carrots, cabbage, celery, onions, garlic, kale, spinach, Romaine lettuce, zucchini, broccoli, etc.). I make a lot of smoothies with my Vitamix blender and fresh greens are a major component. I love kale, celery or spinach added in there. It doesn't affect the taste too much and you're getting all of the amazing phytonutrients, minerals and vitamins that these plants have to offer. It is important to not go to wild with the amount of smoothies one drinks because even though you are consuming whole foods this way, the fiber is broken down so much that it goes right through your system like rocket fuel. It is better to eat the food at a slower pace because of the digestion benefits you get and the improved ability to absorb the nutrients. Also, undigested plant particles that make their way into your gut act as a pre-biotic and help with your gut bacterial flora. The healthy bacteria down there thrive on these undigested particles of plant life and can halt such ailments as leaky gut syndrome.

I eat a modest amount of plant fats in a day, and by modest, I mean maybe an ounce at best. The following is what I tend to consume: ground flax seed, chia seed, sunflower seed, pumpkin seed, walnuts, almonds, pecans, Brazil nuts, avocado and durian. Remember that you are still consuming fat in other sources besides these, so you don't need to worry about getting enough fat in the diet by being prude with your overt plant fat sources. Also, remember to stay clear of vegetable oils. It takes a bit of time to clear that out of the diet but it is possible. For instance, instead of sautéing with oil, use a bit of water or vegetable stock. When it comes to baking my corn bread, I'll use applesauce instead of the egg and the oil. You can also try ground up flax seed with baking. When you grind up flax and add a tiny amount of water it congeals and makes an egg like texture that helps to add that fat component to baked goods, but in a healthier, whole-foods form.

Here are some sample meals that I'll eat throughout the day. I'll add some recipes at the end of the book so you can get an idea of what I do most days. I tend to keep things pretty basic, as I get older. My recipes are not complicated and my taste buds have adjusted to the lower fat, sugar and sodium meals that I create. If something tastes bland to you, add a bit of sugar or salt but if possible try cutting these down and eventually eliminating them from the diet to achieve maximum health benefits.

Breakfast	2 cups of plain oatmeal (oats and hot water) with chopped banana, blueberries, walnuts and cinnamon, 1 glass of water, 2 cups of black coffee and a little cinnamon	The same throughout the week	The same throughout the week	The same throughout the week *maybe banana/blueberry pancakes with maple syrup on occasion
Lunch	Lentil Loaf with mashed potatoes and a	Leftovers from previous meals, or bean	Leftovers or vegetable stir-fry with	Leftovers, or potato cabbage dish with dill and onions or Vegan

	vegetable side (steamed broccoli, asparagus, or kale)	burritos with corn tortillas, black beans, brown rice, potatoes, squash, lettuce, tomato and salsa	broccoli, cauliflower, carrots, snow peas over brown rice	Shepherd's Pie
Dinner	Split pea soup, corn bread and salad	Leftovers, or Red Lentil puree over baked potatoes with side salad of mixed greens, radishes, cherry tomatoes and cucumbers with simple dressing	Leftovers, or Pasta (whole wheat pasta with marinara sauce) side salad and steamed vegetables "zucchini, broccoli"	Leftovers, or vegetable fried rice with salad
Snacks	Smoothies (banana with either orange or pineapple, and spinach or kale.) I use water as a base. Sometimes I add a spoonful of peanut butter, chia seeds or flax seeds	Smoothie or hummus with veggies "carrots, celery"	Smoothie or hummus with veggies or leftovers	Smoothie or hummus with veggies or leftovers

These are just a few "go-to dishes" that I have on hand or make throughout the week. You can get a lot more diverse if you have the time and want to expand your range of options, but this works out great! As you can see I eat a lot of leftovers because when I cook, I cook in volume so that there is always leftover food available for the next day, a later meal, or snack. I may have just some beans for example that I've already cooked for the burritos but I can also add them to my stir-fry in the next meal. If you don't like spending a good chunk of your day in the kitchen, it is great to prepare meals in bulk, so that you can simply heat things up, or toss a few components together to create your lunch or dinner. After some trial and error, you'll discover that it isn't too complicated to make these meals for yourself.

With the exception of some coffee in the morning, I tend to drink the same thing throughout the day, which is plain old water. If I am getting fancy, I'll add bubbles to it with my carbonated water maker. Water is ultimately the best beverage choice. Other drinks may be high in refined carbohydrates that could be bad if you are a person who is trying to lose some weight and needs to really focus on carbohydrates in their whole food form, versus drinking liquid calories in the form of juices or soft drinks. If I drink anything else besides water, it is typically plain soy or almond milk with some whole grain cereal or a beer or two during a social situation. Water wins in most situations though. If you're highly active physically, water should be the go-to drink. I also drink tea during the winter, especially if I'm touring in the Northern parts of the globe where it is ice-cold every day.

I tend to always have the same breakfast of oatmeal and fruit, but occasionally if it is a slow day and I am relaxing a bit, I may make some oil-free pancakes with whatever fruit I have on hand. The diet is not limited to what you see above either. I still go to restaurants and I bend some of my own dietary rules when it comes to oil, salt and sugar (especially in social situations), but there is never a reason for me to bend on the vegan aspect of my lifestyle. There are conflicting views when it comes to moderation but I think it really depends on the individual. Get your blood and urine tested. See how your health is. It may dictate some of your food choices if you have, for example, high cholesterol, high blood pressure or if you have Type 2 Diabetes. You may need to avoid some of these indulgences in order to save your life. If you are healthy, an indulgence once in a while probably won't be a problem.

When people say a vegan diet is luxurious, expensive or something that only rich people can do because you need to shop at all of these high-end grocery stores to pay for organic produce and specialty items, I say that is not true at all. The problem is that most people are in the mindset that the vegan diet is "faux everything" with some vegetables and fruit. You can buy these expensive frozen dinners, veggie burgers, cheeses and yogurts or you can do what I and countless other informed vegans do which is ditch all of that stuff and stick to the produce section and the bulk food section. I wander off occasionally in other parts of the store if I decide to buy some catsup or maple syrup, but generally speaking, I stay only in those two sections.

If you want to find good deals in Los Angeles or if you live outside of LA, seek out discount stores like "99cent Only Store," Mexican or Asian markets. These places usually carry things like rice in bulk and fresh produce at a discounted rate. To get even cheaper and fresher produce, I've lucked out by living near "the produce district" downtown in Los Angeles If you show up there early in the morning, you can buy in bulk, box loads of fresh produce before it heads to restaurants and supermarkets at very low prices. I just bought 40 pounds of ripe bananas today for $5 because they needed to get rid of them and a box of organic blueberries for $5, which I think is 8 pounds. It is so cheap and they need to move their inventory quickly or it spoils, so I'll go home and peel the bananas, freeze them and store them for smoothies. I make use of whatever I can get super cheap and seasonal at the produce district. Check around your city, you may have access to something this cool as well! Also, let me mention the importance of a farmer's market. Let's support these farmers as much as possible. I buy vegetables from the farmer's market every week. I spend only $10-$20 and fill up two bags of fresh, organic, seasonal produce, grown locally. It is amazing and you'll be supporting a group of farmers that tend to care about the quality of their food a lot more so than larger corporate farms. Believe me, you'll taste a difference. An unwaxed apple grown organically and locally tastes so much better than the waxy red delicious you'll get at a conventional grocery store that could have been picked a month ago.

People often want to know how to handle social situations as a vegan. This one is still tough because even though there are more and more people that have adopted this lifestyle, the vast amount of people that I encounter in a day don't have much experience with it. This can make for awkward social situations if you aren't prepared. If you get invited out to a restaurant that isn't vegan, check online first and see if there are any options you can have. If options don't exist on the menu, try calling ahead and ask if you could just order something like a baked potato with nothing on it, steamed vegetables and a salad with only vegetables on it and a wedge of lemon for dressing. This is my go-to for most conventional restaurants, and I'll just eat ahead of time so that I can have any one of the following dishes while enjoying the company of my friends. At first, this may seem like a real pain in the ass, and it is, but as you get used to doing it and you start benefiting in all of the ways you can from this lifestyle, it no longer becomes a big deal.

If you get invited over for dinner, let people know in advance how you eat, that way you don't show up and are expected to eat steak or something similar. I will offer to bring something with me and people are generally ok with this sort of thing. Socially, if I'm in the company of hard-core meat eaters, I just try meeting up with them later on at a bar or something because it's easier for all of us to not have to go through the charade of appeasing each other's dietary choices. I do this only with my fussier friends. Most people I know are fine with my food choices and the way I eat is to be expected, so it doesn't become a major issue.

When it comes time to eating with your meat-eating friends or family, I find it best not to bring up food. Of all the places where it feels inappropriate, the dinner table feels the most inappropriate time and place to have these discussions. In that moment, we're all trying to connect with each other, not sort out our differences. If everyone has something they can eat in front of them, the politics of food will less likely come up. If it does, and you start getting grilled about it, just say you are following something because your doctor recommended a low saturated fat diet and you're trying it out because your family has had heart issues. It is a quick way out of a deep conversation on animal rights or the environmental impact of the animal agriculture industry, which makes people even more uncomfortable when they are sitting there with a big steak on their plate. It is best to have those discussions over coffee or a drink later on if they do come up. I try to be respectful of everyone's thoughts and I hope they are of mine in these situations. It's inevitable though, if you are vegan, you'll have to explain yourself to people now and then. Maybe I can just have them read my book and carry on with life, in the future. ☺

Chapter 9
How to Tour as a Vegan

Getting to a stage in life where you are finally able to travel as a musician is quite a feat. You've spent so much time learning how to write songs and/or play an instrument, that you have made it to a point where you're ready to share it with the world. If you've toured at all, especially the kind of tours that are self-promoted and self-booked, you know all too well how difficult it can be in every way possible. When you're first touring with your band, not many people know who you are or have a reason to care about what you're doing. Chances are, you are pulling this together on a shoestring budget and you've put a lot of your own income into getting your project off the ground in hopes that you'll make a name for yourself, spread your music, sell some merchandise, and maybe make some money off the door to help get you to the next town. This is the harsh reality I faced coming up in the music industry in this day and age.

My first few tours were absolutely brutal. We had our demos and a just a few t-shirts to bring with us. I was going out with this band called Inept from Columbus, Ohio and we were touring with some friends from Cincinnati called Preparation-H. The music was punk rock, for lack of a better way of describing it, and we set out for our adventure in a van that we all chipped in for that cost us about $600. We fixed it up ourselves and hit the road, playing in about 10 cities and college towns around the Midwest. I never traveled much outside of Ohio except for a few vacations to visit family in Philadelphia and New Jersey.

I think being young and full of energy and our dreams of conquering the world had a powerful effect on our reality and touring in this manner had a bit of a romantic vibe to it, starting from the ground up. We crashed on people's floors and sometimes these were squatter houses with no electricity, and sometimes we didn't have a place to crash, so we'd simply drive to the next town and sleep in the van. The conditions were rough. If I remember correctly, we didn't really eat much and health wasn't in our top priority. How many 17 and 18 year olds think about their health and fitness, especially in the punk rock world? Not many. We managed to live off of cheap loaves of bread and peanut butter. If somebody cooked for us, it was typically some spaghetti with cheap tomato sauce. This is pretty bare bones as you can imagine, and the human body can certainly take more abuse than this, but these were certainly harder times and we all were learning on the job.

If you find yourself in this position, which many of you may if you are just starting out on building your career as a touring musician, try to prepare yourself as best as possible. It can be done on a shoestring budget and be almost as healthy as living at home. Being prepared is figuring out your budget first. Calculate your estimated tour costs. Are you all chipping in together? How much money will you make each night from the venue? Was food negotiated with the promoter in advance? Has the band talked about sleeping arrangements and food costs? Is there a per diem for everyone for food? Figure these things out first and then that will dictate what you can do to stay healthy and still follow your dreams. If you start out like I did, you'll be winging it with all of this. We didn't have a clue or any guides to tell us how to do things properly and we learned a lot of lessons the hard way.

Let's assume you have a limited budget. What are some of the essentials to have on you the whole time? If you're traveling in a van or a vehicle without a refrigerator of sorts, you need to have non-perishable items with you that are easy to prepare, affordable, healthy and store well. Your van is going to be subjected to many extreme conditions, mainly heat being the worst. My first few tour vans did not have functioning air conditioning and we could only open the front two windows because these were utility vans, so it gets really hot especially in places like Las Vegas. It is a definite challenge to travel in a van with no A/C, especially in the summer.

My first main suggestion is a big box of quick, rolled oats. Quick, rolled oats are probably the most essential item you can possibly bring with you as far as food goes while on tour. I use them and many of my band mates do, even when I am on a tour bus with a proper kitchen. The thing about quick oats verses steel cut or oat groats, is that they are steamed ahead of time, rolled and then sliced up, causing them to be easily consumed by just adding warm water to them. They are still a whole food, although they are slightly processed. Nutritionally speaking, oat groats in whole form are going to be the best bet, but you'd need at least a microwave and a bit more time to prepare these. Also, your average chain grocery store or convenience store may not carry this unprocessed form of oats all of the time, but I bet you they will have simple quick oats. They are dirt-cheap too, especially if you buy the store brand verses the brand with the "grey haired man" on the cover.

Whether or not you are on a budget, this is a great foundation of your touring diet. I even pack rolled oats in a Ziploc bag and put it in my luggage, so that I am prepared for when I land in another country and have to check into a hotel in the middle of the night. This is so important! You may have just flown for 20 hours and haven't had the chance to hit up a grocery store, so it is good to have food on hand that is ready as soon as you get to a hotel or your destination. You can simply heat up water in a coffee machine in the hotel or if they have a microwave and start going for it. With quick oats, you can even add a bit of regular water or bottled water in countries with non-drinkable tap water to soften your quick oats in a pinch.

Other food items to have on hand are dried fruit. Raisins and prunes tend to be the least expensive dried fruits available, so stock up on these too. You can add them to your oats or eat them as is. Another good compliment to your non-perishable food items is nuts or peanuts (technically a legume), and nut butters. For simplicity, I tend to bring a jar of peanut butter with me or a bag of shelled peanuts. I tend to add either of these items to my oatmeal as well. Just those three ingredients can get you far on your journey with minimal costs. Try not to overdo it with the nuts and dried fruit though. I've found that calorie dense foods like this should never be your staple foods, but act more as a condiment to the main dish, in our case the oats. The reason is that too many nuts will give you too much dietary fat and it will slow you down and may cause heart issues down the line or lead to Type 2 Diabetes if you are consuming too much fat overall.

I feel the same with the amount of dried fruit one should consume. The lack of water in dried fruit gives you a huge spike of sugar without the water buffer and can lead to a quick crash. If you eat these in modest amounts (less than a handful of each) along with the oats, you'll be getting a more natural balance that will give you more sustained energy. With that being said, at all times, you should have these ingredients on hand, especially before flying out to another country, so that you are prepared when you land.

If we stopped right there with these three ingredients and a few raw fruits and vegetables per day, you could tour like this the whole way through. This is always good to fall back on if you're in doubt as to where to spend your limited income.

So you have your oats, dried fruit and nuts. Make sure you have a travel bowl and spoon with you at all times, so that you are prepared. When traveling in a van, you can make this meal at any gas station. Just ask to use the hot water tap that is connected to their coffee maker and simply add hot water to your mixture. Eat this as often as you want I eat a high volume of food but maintain my weight within 10 lbs and have for most of my adult life. Don't worry about overeating these things, especially if the oats are your main source of food. Eat as much as you feel the need to eat. During the day when you are traveling, you're saving up your energy to load your gear, set up, play the show, and load out. All of that physical activity will require a lot of carbohydrates to fuel you.

Always make sure that is the center of your diet. Fruit and whole grains is what you'll need the most of.

After oats, I'd say the next important thing to stock up on is canned foods and cereals. This will add some variety to your diet and if you are still operating with no kitchen or refrigeration, these are foods that can easily be eaten out of the can or the box with minimal effort. It will also give you a little variety that can be helpful to your morale. I am the type of guy that is able to eat the same thing over and over again and be happy, but I know that isn't the case for a lot of people out there, so I have this secondary source of non-perishable items on hand to supplement the food supply. I sometimes buy a large box of vegan cereal or granola and have that on hand as a quick meal idea. If you are able to come across almond/soy milk to eat it with, go for it. You can eat it as is or add juice to it as well. I have dined at many breakfast buffets while on tours that don't carry soy milk, but they have apple juice and orange juice and they have a simple cereal like corn flakes or wheat flakes. I prefer the apple juice in these situations, so go right ahead and make a bowl of cereal. I tend to not drink too many juices and refined foods, but when touring, sometimes you have to make a few exceptions that are not ideal to sustain you while you're on your journey.

As for canned foods, try to buy items low in sodium and without vegetable oils. I tend to buy canned beans because I can add them to the rolled oats and make "tour beans and rice" even though the oats aren't rice. Rice is a bit more involved when it comes to preparation and if you don't have cooking supplies, just rely back on the oats and add some canned beans. While I'm at it, another food morale booster is having some condiments on hand. I tend to pick these up along the way. I enjoy hot sauce and you can make a seemingly boring meal a bit more exciting by putting a little hot sauce on it. Hot sauces tend to be non-perishable too, so you can bring them out and not worry about them going bad. Add them to your beans or whatever else you like.

Another tip for traveling on a very low budget while being vegan with a focus on positive health is to buy fresh produce when you can. When you stop at a grocery store or even a truck stop, see if there are any fresh fruits or vegetables you can pick up, wash easily and consume right away. I have been known over the years to buy a head of kale which tends to be about a dollar or two, wash it in the bathroom and chew on it as we head to the next town. It is challenging to get fresh vegetables in your diet when traveling around the country each day and maybe eating things like raw kale sounds a bit progressive, but try it. Your body will thank you and it will help round out your diet while focusing mostly on non-perishable starches. If you simply can't do kale, try buying celery, carrots, lettuce, spinach, cherry tomatoes, apples, oranges, berries, grapes, or whatever you can that is affordable. Try to incorporate some raw fruits and vegetables into your diet daily. I simply wash and start eating. If you have the budget and the ability, you can even make some salads with all the fresh produce. A lot of stores also carry those microwavable rice packs that are fairly inexpensive. You can make a salad, add the rice and squeeze a bit of lemon or orange juice on top and make a full meal. There are so many possibilities depending on your touring conditions.

If your conditions and budget are more forgiving, there are a few tools that you can add to your arsenal. On one of my early tours with Mankind Is Obsolete I brought with me a pot and a hot plate. This helped us save a ton of money in the long run and we probably ate a lot better than hitting up fast food chains each day. Some of our meals may not have been the healthiest, but you can do so much with a hot plate and a pot. I can recall making Top-Ramen "Oriental Flavor," the only vegan flavor, in the pot with a hot plate. I think we cut up cabbage and threw it in the ramen noodle soup to keep things dirt cheap and exciting! I'm pretty sure I fed a band of 5 people for under $2. These days we have the amazing ability to access information online, and so it is easy to find a million recipes for simple one-pot vegan meals. Type that in your search engine and I'm sure it will fuel you with many ideas that I didn't have access to back in the day.

Now that you have a hot plate and a pot you can buy potatoes and rice! Potatoes and rice are readily available pretty much everywhere and they are both super cheap! Think about all the different parts of the world that live or have lived on diets where rice or potatoes were, or are still, the staple food. In Asia, rice is still a huge component of the diet and is consumed during most meals. In South America and many parts of Europe and Russia, potatoes have been a staple and primary food source that has fueled civilizations of people.

Go to a discount grocery store and buy a 10 lb bag of potatoes and the biggest bag of brown rice you can find. White rice is fine too, especially while on tour. White rice can be made a lot quicker, but brown rice is superior as far as healthy choices go. You'll be getting the fiber and some vitamins that will no longer be present in the white rice. In the recipe section, I'll show you a few ideas you can try with these as your staple, such as one pot veggies, beans and rice, or tour boiled potatoes. With just these simple foods, you can make so many quick meals by simply adding a can of beans and a few vegetables or even just one vegetable if that is all you have. Throw some hot sauce on it and Voila! You have a healthy meal that you could have prepared at home and you can feed your whole band and crew on it for just a few bucks!

I have been the band chef before and created plenty of simple dishes that focused on a starch and a vegetable, sometimes with beans added to it. Another thing you can do instead of buying a hot plate and a pot is to buy a rice cooker. There are rice cookers for $20 out there and most of them work really well and they make rice really fast. I have recently been touring a lot in Europe with IAMX, and I left my rice cooker at our storage unit in Germany because I think we'll be touring mostly out there. One easy meal idea is to also buy some cheap vegetables to add to your cooked rice. For simplicity's sake, you can simply add a few chopped vegetables into the rice cooker when you're cooking the rice and it will all come out as a pretty good meal that is cheap. Use hot sauce, soy sauce or salsa as a condiment and you're set. I can't tell you how many times we were sitting on the bus with a day off and we all opted to use the rice cooker for steamed veggies and rice over going out to a restaurant. You'll eat so much better and save a ton of cash.

Not only is this way of eating more affordable than fast food or prepackaged meals, it's a lot healthier too because you're not going to have all of that added fat or sodium that is in fast food or prepackaged meals. I love and have benefitted from eating this way so much that I eat pretty much like this when I am not on tour as well. You can get as creative as you'd like but I tend to keep things simple because of my tastes and convenience. Additionally, even when you graduate to a tour bus, space tends to always be an issue. You need to buy things more often because the storage is limited, and you may only be able to store a few dried goods at a time.

If your band is doing better, your contracts with venues may be better as well, and food may be worked into the equation. If this is the case, talk to the manager and let him/her know about your vegan diet. This goes for flights too. A lot of international flights serve meals and pretty much every airline has a vegan option. I've had a few good meals on some of these airlines too. The passenger sitting next to me usually becomes more interested in my meal then whatever they are serving to the general public. I've had bean burritos with brown rice and vegetables, pasta with marinara sauce, tofu and vegetable stir fry over rice, to name a few. Usually all of these meals come with a small salad, fruit and a dessert that is also vegan, so definitely plan these days ahead to guarantee you'll be set. If you show up within 24 hours of your flight, they may not be able to accommodate your special meal so be proactive and make sure you are set.

Also, when the manager knows, he/she can inform the booking agent who will be negotiating deals with promoters. A lot of times you'll get vegan meals prepared for you backstage along with a fruit, vegetable and sandwich spread for food during the day while you're loading in and sound checking. Always gather some of that food at the end of the day and put it in storage containers. You may never have to shop if you bring that loaf of bread, cereal, soy milk and leftover fruits and vegetables. There are times when a promoter or a venue has no idea what a vegan meal is, or you're in a city where veganism isn't very well recognized and they may give you a "buy-out" instead. A buy-out is simply money that was going to go towards your meal that will go directly into your pocket instead and you'll have to fend for yourself.

In these cases of fending for yourself, or if the promoter is in a bind trying to get you vegan meal, you can help guide them in the right direction. When in doubt, I tell them they can order a pizza without cheese and lots of vegetables on top. I will usually get a side salad with no dressing as well. This can be ordered from many different pizza establishments and most crusts and sauces are vegan. You can have them check or go online and look up the ingredients. A lot of major chain pizza places have vegan options. You'd be surprised at how many major chains can accommodate you. I believe that PETA has an online guide on how to veganize your order from a major chain.

I am usually happy with a buy-out as long as I have my rice cooker, or if the venue has a microwave or a means to cook some food myself. I'll just steam a lot of rice and add some vegetables and beans. This is a go-to for me. I can eat this every day and feel fine. Also, because of the lightness of this food, I think you'll perform better as well. If you've ever gone on stage after gorging yourself with a rich meal like veggie burgers and fries, you'll feel like garbage when you hit the stage and may even puke depending on the amount of time you've had to digest and how intense of a performer you are. I've nearly puked a few times from eating a rich and heavy meal only an hour before going on stage. It is best to eat your last meal about 2 to 2 ½ hours before you go on stage and make sure it isn't a massive meal. Save that for after the show if you need to. Eat some fruit if you need calories as the show nears, or if you're experiencing hunger pains. Also, stay hydrated with water. That is key as well.

Being on tour is quite jarring and it can really wear you out, especially if you go at it for months on end. It is important to stay physically fit in order to put on the best possible performance each night. I recommend adding a bit of endurance training to go along with your vegan diet. When I am at home, I have the luxury of my gym, bicycle and pool, but when on tour, I need to strip things down to the basics. You will get some exercise just by loading gear in and out of the club as well as performing the show, but this amount of exercise can really vary depending on the style of music, the size of your crew helping out, how many shows you have and how long your set is. I've spent so many years touring as an opening band that only gets a half hour set each night. This can be intense, but when you become a headliner, you're expected to play for about 90 minutes. However, because I am a multi-instrumentalist who mostly plays electronic music, I have toured a few times with more than one band on the same tour and as many as 3 bands on one particular tour. I definitely got a workout during that time!

All that being said, try to get about 30 minutes of endurance training in per day whenever possible. I usually do this 5 or 6 days per week while on tour, but also make sure you have at least one rest day per week. That is equally important. You don't want to burn yourself out but you do want to be in peak physical form. Some activities I do are running, push-ups, sit-ups or crunches, squats, lunges and if I am running around town, I will try to find a park because they have monkey bars or other structures where you can do pull-ups, chin-ups and dips. You don't need a gym and you can get pretty creative with this. While I am at it, bring a bathing suit with you. You'll often stay at hotels and they usually have a pool, and sometimes an indoor pool as well and you can wake up in the morning and swim laps for a bit. I find this to be the most enjoyable since I grew up as a swimmer and diver. It is also a great form of cardiovascular exercise mixed with strength training and is easy on all of your joints. I think swimming is one of the top exercises for humans at all ages, no matter what your physical fitness level is. I've even had the luxury on occasion to be right next to an ocean. I'll usually take advantage of swimming in it during the summer months if I can manage to fit it in.

So my routine looks a bit like this. You'll probably have a "day sheet" or a schedule for each day and so you can see where you can fit in a 30-minute workout. I try to also center it on my ability to take a shower. Maybe the band is extremely grimy though and that won't matter, but when I can, I like to be presentable. I spend a good amount of my days being dirty from drumming and other physical activity. I like to do a workout maybe after dinner but before the show because it also gets me warmed-up to play. I may just jog around the venue and explore the city a bit. It is a good way to do two things at once. I bring my cell phone with me so I can stop and take a picture while I am out. After all, you're getting paid to travel; one of the perks is experiencing a different city, which may have some amazing sites. Also, jogging like this gives me a little "alone time" which can help reset things a bit. We all get crammed in a van, bus and sometimes a hotel room together and it is nice to have little moments of space. This is the easiest no-brainer activity you can do to help with endurance while on tour. Simply start jogging, running or even walking. Add in a few push-ups, squats and sit-ups for a better-rounded workout. I like to try to do at least 50 of each along with my jog, and I find that it keeps me in pretty good shape during the tour. You can do more if you'd like, or less if you are not used to a lot of endurance training, but try it if you can. The side effects are all good. You'll feel better, look better, perform better, and it will help you to stay healthy on the road. Many people get very sick on tour because one minute you're in a muggy club, the next minute you may be out in the freezing rain. Add a less than ideal diet, little sleep and maybe a bit of boozing, and sickness becomes a problem on most tours. It usually starts with one person and when it happens, it typically gets us all at some point. If you can make it through without getting sick, you'll be a lot happier.

One last thing on working out: during days off, I like to explore a city. Don't take a cab or a bus out to points of interest. Get out and walk! If you walk all day long and set out for maybe 2 different sites, you may get in 5-10 miles of walking which is plenty of physical activity for the day. I think this is a better use of my time. I save money and I get to explore a new city or site. Also, walking is pretty low impact yet it keeps you in shape. Touring conditions are rough but we usually at least have some energy to walk around a bit.

There are other things you can do to train while on the road. Bring a resistance band or some collapsible weights where you just add water to them. There are a number of strength workouts you can do with these little pieces of gear, and they fit in your carry-on luggage. I have resistance bands that I always bring with me and so if it is a rainy day outside, maybe I'll do a workout in the dressing room while the other bands are sound checking. The key is to be flexible and be prepared.

As I mentioned before when you aren't touring, sleep is another key component to any healthy lifestyle. I am a light sleeper and touring can really be a challenge for me in regards to proper sleep. It isn't always possible to get a solid seven or eight hours of sleep, so on days off, really try to let your body recover and sleep a bit more. Take a nap if you need to while others are sound checking. If you have a bus, just go out to the bus and sleep in your bunk for 20 minutes while someone else is line-checking his/her instrument with the sound engineer.

If you tour regularly like I do, in order to keep this lifestyle up, you can't pull off all of the rock n' roll clichés and last too long. There are certainly anomalies out there who drink, do lots of drugs, have sex with tons of groupies and still get up each day to kick ass on stage, but that is certainly not me. I have had my crazy rock moments and it wiped me out and made me not perform as well as I could. Maybe it's because I'm a drummer, I feel the need to keep it all together each night. If I mess up or lose my place, the whole band can be derailed, and I've certainly caused a couple of train wrecks in my time. It's embarrassing, even if it was something beyond my control, such as my in-ear monitors not functioning properly and then all of the sudden I'm not hearing the band properly and the whole thing caves in. That is something you can't do much about, but putting on a bad show because you are hung over is inexcusable for someone in my position. Most of the time, I am hired on to a tour and I simply don't have the ability to behave in these cliché ways and still have gigs locked in. The leaders of the bands can certainly have a bit more wiggle room with some of their lifestyle choices and maybe in some cases it is to be expected for a leader to live out some rock n' roll clichés so others can vicariously live through them. The bands are theirs, and they set a bar as to how others can behave, but it's still a good idea to keep things in check a bit for your own sake. It's totally fun to reap the rewards of getting to tour on a larger scale, where there are tons of partying opportunities. In my case, though, I had to limit those moments to special occasions and I am quite happy to do so. Hangovers are not worth it for me.

It is important to be able to relax and have fun after a show or on a day off with your band mates, but use a bit of discretion when it comes to doing things that could ruin your gig. Just don't be a douche bag if you are in a hired gun situation like I normally am. Some bands thrive on their antics and it becomes more about that than the music. I know from personal experience that most bands don't last behaving in this manner. This isn't the 80's anymore, for better or worse. Be careful with the clichés. Who knows though? We all need to figure this stuff out for ourselves.

Chapter 10
Assimilating in the World While Being Vegan

I'll be the first to admit that vegans get a reputation for being sanctimonious assholes by the general public because we now are sitting in judgment of other people's lifestyle choices since we stopped eating animals. This may be true in many cases (and has been even in my own case), but it is important to remember a few things. For starters, we all hate to be judged and told what to do, especially from a stranger who doesn't know our backgrounds. It is common for us all to cringe when approached by a religious zealot on the street that wants us to convert right away for our salvation. We all know that doesn't work for people who make intelligent decisions for themselves. The same goes for veganism. I attended many animal rights protests and have done my share of leafleting when I was younger, and I know that I got a lot more retaliation from others than support. It is an uphill battle to convert people to this way of thinking. I try to remember what got me here in the first place. It was having pets that I loved and my desire to protect them and give them a good life. It was fishing with my uncle and having to filet the fish that we caught. It was watching "Faces of Death" which graphically showed slaughterhouse footage, fur farms and the torture of animals. It was my father's depression and eventual suicide that made me want to minimize my own suffering and the suffering of others around me. This helped me not only be vegan for the animals but to also look out for the groups of people in life that get bullied around by more dominating forces.

These instances in life are what lead me to a vegan lifestyle. It wasn't because of a protester. Everyone is different and will gather his or her own life's moral code. I think that I have had the most affect for other animals and people is by doing this long term and sharing it now. As with most people in the world, we surround ourselves with a diverse group of people, whether by choice or not, and we have to learn to try to understand why people choose different paths. It seems conflicting because on one hand, how does this help the animals by keeping your mouth shut? On the other hand, we know that preaching generally turns people off. I've found that people usually like to discover things for themselves. The best thing we can do to get an idea across is to be a shining example of what we believe in. This is why I focus on health so much. Not only is my constant quest for understanding the human body and what is best for it good for me, it is also good for the message I'd like to share with the world. If I am a healthy guy and appear that way, I am doing the vegan message a good service. We all see sick looking people out there that are out of shape and have self-inflicted health disorders. If those people are claiming they are long-term vegans as I do, then it looks bad for vegans as a whole. We're a niche group and people will judge us, and the vegan lifestyle, based on our attitudes and appearance.

I feel that if I present this lifestyle in a way that is relatively easy to adjust to and proven to be healthy, as new scientific data confirms, I will naturally affect those around me in a positive way. I remember being involved in the hard-core scene back in the early 90's and seeing so many vegans that it helped me push over to doing so myself. I already was upset with the way we treat animals and didn't want to partake in the systematic suffering of these intelligent beings and seeing a few other teenagers and young adults making it happen made me think, "If they can do it, so can I."

So with this being said, we all pick our paths and we all have our own moral code. Others may disagree with my approach and that is fine. There will never be a shortage of dogmatic people out there who are armed with facts and ready to argue. Those people have an effect. Sometimes the effect is positive, and sometimes it turns people off. My approach is different. I think this is why the word "vegan" has been taboo lately. More people have been using the term "plant-based" for this reason. I think they don't want to associate with all of the negative baggage of the word "vegan." It is all the same to me, but I understand this. I'm hesitant to tell people I am vegan at times because I feel it instantly puts up a wall between me and whoever I am speaking with, The person on the other end may think I am judging them (and they're right), but I try to be polite.

When it really comes down to it, veganism should be something that all people think is a positive thing. At its core, it's about treating others (animals included) with respect, respecting one's self and respecting the environment. What's bad about that? These are people that have a good heart and want to do something good for the planet and its inhabitants. The same goes for religious zealots. I think this is why people look at veganism as a religion or a cult at times. Even though that isn't true, veganism has some of the same negative parallels to organized religion. I'm sure most people that feel strongly about their religion have good intentions, but we see around us what happens when they take to the streets with it, or pass judgment onto others who don't follow their way.

Be a shining example. I really think this is the best way to do things. I think you'll win over a lot more people if you respect your body while respecting the animals. Take care of yourself with healthy, whole, plant-based food, exercise, get enough sleep and try to focus on the positive aspects of your life. You'll be an undeniable force.

Chapter 11
How I Eat While Touring

A lot of what you make on tour depends on what sort tools you bring with you on the road. If you have nothing at all you can always make a few simple things. Here are some staples to have on hand:

Rolled oats (quick oats)

A jar of peanut butter

A box of low sodium crackers

A loaf of sprouted grain bread

Dried fruit (raisins, currants, banana chips, apricots, cranberries)

A bag of nuts (walnuts, peanuts, pecans, almonds)

Canned beans (oil-free refried, vegan baked beans, or plain beans)

Microwaveable rice or quinoa packets

Dr. McDougall or Engine 2 convenience foods (available at health food stores)

If I have absolutely no tools on hand, I make meals using the above ingredients. You can absolutely pull together a meal while driving using any of these items minus the oats. I heat the oats at truck stops with their coffee maker hot water dispenser. Stop at grocery stores whenever possible to grab simple raw fruits or vegetables to supplement your diet. I also recommend canned beans that have a lid that you can simply pull off and microwavable rice packets. You can easily put together beans and rice, which is a perfect meal.

If you have a rice cooker or a pot and hot plate you can do so much more. In these cases, I get bags of brown rice and lentils because they don't require as much time as other beans to cook. All you need to do to cook these in the rice cooker is to add a 2:1 ratio of water to lentils or brown rice. My main dish is to also add chopped vegetables to this during the last 5-10 minutes of cooking. I simply cut up carrots, broccoli, cauliflower, squash, sweet potatoes, collard greens, cabbage or kale and add that to the rice cooker while you're steaming the rice and or lentils and that is a meal. Bring some hot sauce along or anything else you'd like to add to it and you have a complete meal. With vegan meals that are low in fat with no added oils, it is easy for me to take down two plates of food. That is fine because it still will end up most likely having fewer calories than your average fast food meal with tons of grease and processed ingredients.

To recap a typical day on tour, I'll start off in the morning eating oatmeal and fruit. This can be done at the breakfast bar of a hotel, or in your tour van or bus. Just get hot water at truck stops, the hotel lobby, or tour buses usually have hot water boilers and microwaves. If you need to have a heavier breakfast, add some peanut butter or chopped nuts or seeds to the oatmeal.

For lunch while either traveling or arriving at the venue, it will usually be peanut butter sandwiches with raw vegetables that I'll buy along the way, hummus sandwiches with lettuce and tomatoes,\. If I'm not traveling at the time, I'll use the rice cooker to heat up rice with vegetables or poke a few holes with a fork into some potatoes or sweet potatoes and place them in the rice cooker with a small amount of water to steam them. Dinner is usually similar to lunch, or if I have the ability order food, it will be something from a local vegan restaurant such as vegan Pad Thai, vegan pizza or vegan burgers with a salad. I try to limit my eating out because of the added oil and salt that most restaurants use. Sometimes it is unavoidable though when I am not prepared.

When it comes to snacks, I prefer to have fruit such as dates, bananas, apples, oranges or grapes, vegetables such as carrots, broccoli, celery, cauliflower, or cereal with unsweetened almond milk. When I'm out with IAMX we are all way into eating oatmeal or whole grain cereal with almond milk and berries. That seems to be something we all regularly consume. It's easy to prepare, and when everyone is eating the same thing, we'll use up the berries and almond milk quickly so that it won't go bad in the event that we can't refrigerate it.

Get creative though and try a few different things. I seem to stick to a routine but occasionally I need to stray from that and add some variety to my diet. I'm generally happy with keeping things simple and uncomplicated.

Chapter 12
Recipes While At Home
Preparing For Tour

Oatmeal

2 cups of quick oats
1 banana
1 handful of berries (blueberries, blackberries, etc.)
1 spoonful of nuts or nut butter (peanuts, walnuts, pecans, etc.)
½ teaspoon of cinnamon
3 cups of water (this can vary by a ½ cup depending on
how creamy you like your oats)

*Start off by boiling the water in a kettle and then just pour the hot water over all of the ingredients in the bowl. You can also pour the water, cinnamon, banana, and oats in a bowl and microwave it for 2 minutes and then add the remaining ingredients.

**Also, if adjusting to eating oatmeal without any sweetener added is tough, try a spoonful of real maple syrup or agave after you cook the oats.

Smoothies

The Tropical Dream:

4 frozen bananas
2 cups of pineapple
1 handful of spinach
2 cups of water

*Add all ingredients to a high-powered blender and pulse away!

**You can use non-frozen bananas if you'd like and add a couple of ice cubes too.

***bananas should always be consumed "ripe" meaning yellow with black spots on them. They are too starchy and may not digest well if they are green or yellow without spots. Also, be sure to peel the bananas before freezing them.

The Classic PB and B

4 frozen bananas
1 large spoonful of "natural" peanut butter

2 cups of water
1 scoop of chocolate vegan protein powder
(optional)

*Add all ingredients to a high-powered blender and pulse
away!

**You can use non-frozen bananas if you'd like and add a
couple of ice cubes too.

***Bananas should always be consumed "ripe" meaning
yellow with black spots on them. They are too starchy and
may not digest well if they are green or yellow without
spots. Also, be sure to peel the bananas before freezing
them.

****Protein powder isn't really necessary on a vegan diet
as long as you get enough calories from whole food
sources.

Soups

Split Pea Soup

1 bag of split peas (green or yellow)
1 onion, diced
2 carrots, diced
2 celery sticks, diced
2 medium sized potatoes, diced
1 TBSP garlic powder
2 TBSP dill
1 Bay Leaf
2 tablespoons of rolled oats
Water
A pinch of salt and pepper if desired

*Start with a big pot and a ¼ cup of water. Bring the water to boil and add chopped vegetables and sauté for 5 minutes, stirring regularly. Add the bag of split peas and spices. Stir for 30 seconds and then fill up the pot with water until the water covers the contents by 3 inches. Bring to a boil and then once you are at a boil, bring the temperature down to a low setting and simmer for 1 hour or until the peas are soft. Keep a lid on the pot but check often so that it doesn't boil over. Stir often. After about an hour, add the oats and then blend with a soup blender or carefully add a small amount of the soup into your blender. You can blend small amounts at a low speed. Be careful to have things at a low speed if you are using a standard blender because the hot soup can easily explode everywhere. If the blender has a plastic top on the rubber lid, crack it open to release some of the hot air while blending. This will lower your chances of being sprayed with hot soup! Add salt, pepper if desired, to taste. I add just a small amount "roughly ½ tsp" because my palate is accustomed to lower sodium meals, but you can add a bit more if you need it. This makes a lot of soup, enough for friends or leftovers. It goes well with corn bread or sprouted whole grain bread and a salad.

Brown Lentil Soup
16oz bag of brown lentils
1 onion, diced
2 carrots, diced
2 celery sticks, diced
2 medium sized potatoes, diced
1 TBSP of garlic powder
1 TBSP Thyme
1 TBSP of Rosemary
1 TBSP of Basil
1 Bay Leaf
A pinch of salt and pepper
Water

*Start with a big pot and a ¼ cup of water. Bring the water to boil and add chopped vegetables and sauté for 5 minutes, stirring regularly. Add the bag of brown lentils and spices. Stir for 30 seconds and then fill up the pot with water until the water covers the contents with 3 inches of water above. Bring to a boil and then once you are at a boil, bring the temperature down to a low setting and simmer for 45 minutes to 1 hour or until the lentils are soft. Keep a lid on the pot but check often so that it doesn't boil over. Stir often. This soup works well pureed or partially pureed or as is, so I sometimes will add a few ladles of the soup into a blender on a very low speed, so you don't get burned, and add that back into the pot. Like all of the soup recipes, a nice bread and salad pair up well with this and they'll be plenty for leftovers.

Borscht (Beet Soup):

1 bunch of beets with greens attached
1 onion diced
2 carrots shredded or diced
1 half head of green cabbage
1 TBSP garlic powder
2 TBSP dill
1 Bay Leaf
1 lemon, juiced
A pinch of salt and pepper
Water
1 cup of cooked butter lima beans (optional)

*Start with a big pot and a ¼ cup of water. Bring the water to a boil and add chopped onions and sauté for 2 minutes, stirring frequently. Next add shredded or diced beets, (save the beet greens for later) shredded or diced carrots, garlic powder, dill, bay leaf and a pinch of salt and pepper.

Sautee about a minute longer, stirring regularly. Add 5-6 cups of water and bring the mixture to a boil and then lower the heat down to a simmer and stir now and then. Keep the pot covered when you're not stirring and cook for 15 minutes while simmering. Add shredded cabbage and cook for 5 more minutes. Add shredded beet greens and cooked lima beans (optional) and simmer for another 5 minutes. Add the juice of the lemon and then turn off the heat. If you need more salt or pepper, add. If you are looking for a heartier soup you can add the beans, but I don't find it necessary. I recall having borscht while living in Poland during a summer and occasionally we'd add these large beans to it to make a more satisfying meal, along with dark buckwheat bread.

Main Dishes

Oven Baked Potatoes or Sweet Potatoes

3 lbs (or around 7) medium potatoes or sweet potatoes

*Preheat oven to 400F. Chop up the potatoes or sweet potatoes into bite-sized cubes, removing any brown spots. Using a silicone pan liner and a baking sheet, spread the cubed potatoes or sweet potatoes until the sheet is full. A silicone pan liner is a great non-stick surface so that you won't have to use oil for this recipe. If you don't have one, lightly oil the surface of a baking sheet and lay the cubed potatoes or sweet potatoes on top. Bake the potatoes for 25 to 30 minutes, or until you can easily put a fork through the potato/sweet potato. Bake longer if you prefer a bit more of a crispy surface. Remove from heat and use this as a foundation for a recipe. I like this with red lentil sauce and steamed asparagus/broccoli or a side salad. It is also good with a lentil loaf.

Mashed Potatoes or Sweet Potatoes

3 lbs (or around 7) medium sized potatoes or
sweet potatoes
Water
Garlic powder (optional)
Salt and pepper (optional)

*Wash and remove any brown spots on the
potatoes/sweet potatoes. Chop the potatoes/sweet
potatoes into quarters. Using a large pot, fill the pot with
the potatoes/sweet potatoes and then cover them with
water. Put a lid on the pot. Bring the water and
potatoes/sweet potatoes to a boil and then lower the heat
to a simmer. Cook for around 20 minutes or until the
potatoes are tender enough that you can easily pierce
them with a fork. Drain most of the water, reserving
about 2 cups of water and smash the potatoes/sweet
potatoes mixed with water, with a potato masher. Add
garlic powder, salt and pepper to taste if desired. This is
great with lentil loaf and steamed greens. It is also great
with cooked beans and a side salad.

Brown Rice, Quinoa or any other whole grain

1 cup whole grain
2 cups water

*Put 1 cup of your favorite grain (millet, brown rice, quinoa, wheat berries, barley, etc.) and 2 cups of water into pot with a lid. Bring this to a boil, and turn down the heat to a low simmer and cook for 10-30 minutes depending on the grain. Keep the lid on during the simmering process and check periodically so that it doesn't boil over in a frothy mess. The water will no longer be seen on the top when the grain is properly cooked. Turn off the heat and allow it to sit for 5 minutes with the lid still on before serving.

**You can also use a rice cooker for any of these grains and do the 2 to 1 water to grain ratio. Some rice cookers come with a steamer function and I will add chopped vegetables to it to create a complete meal of steamed vegetables and brown rice.

Eastern European Potato and Cabbage Dish

4 medium sized potatoes
½ head of green cabbage
1 small onion or ½ large onion
1 tsp garlic powder
½ tsp black pepper
1 TBSP dried dill
¼ cup apple cider vinegar (optional)

*Dice the potatoes (I leave the skins on, but remove brown spots), shred the cabbage and dice the onions. Add a ½ cup of water to a large nonstick pot and turn the heat on high until the water starts to simmer. Add the contents to the pot and stir occasionally for 5 minutes. Add another ½ cup of water to the mix and put a lid on the pot. Bring down the heat to medium-low and allow it to gently simmer for 20 minutes. Stir often and add additional water if it becomes really dry at the bottom of the pot. If using salt, add a pinch or two before you put the lid on it. Add vinegar if using it during the last 5 minutes and stir some more. The potatoes should be able to be easily pierced with a fork. Then you'll know it is done. Serve this as a main dish with a side salad or some soup.

Easy steamed vegetables

Any vegetable you like: (carrots, cauliflower, broccoli, zucchini, yellow squash, kale, collard greens, asparagus, etc.)

*Chop as many vegetables as you want to consume. I usually cut enough to fill half of a pot. I add about a cup of water, or enough to create a ½ inch of water at the bottom of the pot. I bring this to a boil and then add the chopped vegetables into the pot and put a lid on it. At this point lower the heat to medium. I start with the heartier vegetables. They will take longer to steam (carrots, yams, turnips, etc.) If you are making these, let them steam for about 15 minutes or until they are "fork tender." If you're mixing things up and adding an array of vegetables, add broccoli and squash next maybe 10 minutes into cooking the harder vegetables. Lastly, add any leafy greens during the last 5 minutes. It should only take about 5 minutes to steam leafy greens. It is a matter of taste too. If you prefer the vegetables to be extra soft, leave them in there for another 5 minutes or so and always check to see if there is still some water at the bottom of the pot to help create the steam. Steamed vegetables are perfect on their own, or you can add a little lemon juice, hot sauce, fat-free salad dressing, or tomato sauce to them if you'd like to add some zazz to them.

Red Lentil Sauce

1 cup of red lentils
2 cups of water
1 small onion
1 TBSP dried basil
1 tsp of black pepper
1 tsp of garlic powder
1 cup of soy milk (or water)
2 TBSP of flour, arrowroot powder or corn starch

*Add your lentils and water to a small pot with a lid. Bring to a boil and then reduce heat to a simmer and let simmer until the red lentils are cooked all the way through and most of the water gets absorbed or evaporates. This should take about 15 minutes. Keep an eye on the pot. This can easily boil over, so reduce heat to a gentle simmer. In a separate pot, water sauté the chopped onion in ¼ cup of water for 5 minutes, stirring often on med-high heat. Next add the basil, pepper and garlic powder to the mix. Add a pinch of salt if you desire at this stage. Pour in the lentils from the pot and add the soymilk or water to the mix and allow this to gently begin to boil. Make sure the heat isn't too high. It can easily boil over. Stir for about 5 minutes or so until it is gently simmering. Next stir in the flour, arrowroot or corn starch. A trick you can do is to take out a bit of the mixture and stir the starch into it before returning it to the pot. This will help break up the fine powdery corn starch. Let the entire pot simmer for just a couple of minutes longer and you should have a nice, rich lentil sauce. I use this sauce for everything! I pour it over baked potatoes. You can have it with quinoa or brown rice. You can eat it with some sprouted grain bread like a stew. It is a versatile dish.

Simple Stir Fry:

5 cups of any vegetable you enjoy, chopped

½ cup vinegar (Any kind will do.)
½ cup of soy sauce, Bragg's liquid aminos, Nama Shoyu, or tamari
1 TBSP of thickening starch (corn starch, arrowroot, or flour)
1 TBSP of garlic powder
1 tsp maple syrup (optional)
1 TBSP sriracha or hot sauce (optional)

*Chop your vegetables up and fire up a wok or a large pot on high. Add a ¼ cup of water and let it begin to simmer. Add your chopped vegetables (I like onion, broccoli, snap peas, carrots, cauliflower, zucchini squash, bok choy) and stir often for the next 5 minutes on high. Bring the temperature down a bit to medium and add a lid to the pot or wok. This will help create some steam and cook the vegetables all the way through. I cook them for 5-10 minutes longer. While this is going, I combine the other ingredients in a separate bowl and stir them up so that the thickening agent dissolves into the solution. Pour this over the vegetables inside the wok and let it simmer again for another 5 minutes, stirring often. Serve over brown rice, millet or quinoa.

Baked Tofu

1 block of extra firm tofu
2 TBSP Tamari or Soy Sauce
1 tsp garlic powder
1/4 tsp black pepper

*Preheat your oven to 400F. Drain and pat dry the tofu with some paper towels. Slice into ¼ inch rectangles and marinade in the remaining ingredients. If you have time, you can do this step and leave the tofu overnight in the refrigerator to create a more flavorful baked tofu. Next, lay the tofu on a non-stick baking sheet and bake for 15 minutes. Flip tofu on the other side and bake for 10 more minutes. Remove from the oven and let it cool for a few minutes before chopping up into tiny cubes. The baked tofu can be used as a main course with BBQ sauce, mashed potatoes and steamed vegetables or added to a salad. You can also avoid the "cubing" step and simply cool the tofu off in the refrigerator and use it for sandwiches. Just add lettuce, tomato, red onions, mustard etc. and enjoy it between two slices of toasted, sprouted-grain bread.

Salads and Dressings

Entrée Salad

1 head of romaine lettuce
1 leaf of kale (stem removed)
1 tomato
¼ avocado
¼ red onion or 2 green onions sliced thin
2 radishes
½ cup of leftover brown rice, quinoa and/or beans

*Chop all of the ingredients up. Toss the leftover rice, quinoa and/or beans on top (chilled) and then add any oil-free dressing you'd like!

Simple AF Dressing

¼ apple cider or balsamic vinegar
1 TBSP of stone ground mustard
1 TBSP of real maple syrup

*Stir and put over your salad!

Citrus Cashew Dressing

 1 orange juiced
5-10 cashews

*In a blender, blend the ingredients until it is delightfully creamy and add to your salad.

Guacamole Dressing

 ½ avocado
5 limes juiced
1 clove of garlic

*Blend the ingredients and pour over your salad.